Drugs: Policy and Politics

INTRODUCING SOCIAL POLICY
Series Editor: David Gladstone

Published titles

Perspectives on Welfare
Alan Deacon

Risk, Social Policy and Welfare
Hazel Kemshall

Comparative Social Policy: Theory and Research
Patricia Kennett

Education in a Post-Welfare Society
Sally Tomlinson

Social Security and Welfare
Robert Walker

Reconceptualizing Social Policy
Amanda Coffey

Education in a Post-Welfare Society: Second edition
Sally Tomlinson

Drugs: Policy and Politics

Edited by

RHIDIAN HUGHES, RACHEL LART
and PAUL HIGATE

Open University Press

Open University Press
McGraw-Hill Education
McGraw-Hill House
Shoppenhangers Road
Maidenhead
Berkshire
England
SL6 2QL

email: enquiries@openup.co.uk
world wide web: www.openup.co.uk

and Two Penn Plaza, New York, NY 10121-2289, USA

First published 2006

A catalogue record of this book is available from the British Library

ISBN-10: 0 335 21616 1 (pbk)   0 335 21617 X (hbk)
ISBN-13: 978 0 335 21616 1 (pbk)   978 0 335 21617 8 (hbk)

Library of Congress Cataloging-in-Publication Data
CIP data has been applied for

Typeset by RefineCatch Limited, Bungay, Suffolk
Printed in Poland by OZGraf S.A.
www.polskabook.pl

Contents

Series Editor's Foreword

Welcome to the seventh volume in the Introducing Social Policy series. The series itself is designed to provide a range of well informed texts on a wide variety of topics that fall within the ambit of social policy studies.

Although primarily designed with undergraduate social policy students in mind, it is hoped that the series – and individual titles within it – will have a wider appeal to students in other social science disciplines and to those engaged on professional and post-qualifying courses in health care and social welfare.

The aim throughout the planning of the series has been to produce a series of texts that both reflect and contribute to contemporary thinking and scholarship, and which present their discussion in a readable and easily accessible format.

Drug use and misuse frequently makes the headlines and, as this collection of essays shows, drug issues are an important interstice between social policy, health and medicine, law and criminal justice. It is all the more surprising, therefore, that the discussion of drug users and drug policy in social policy studies has hitherto been disparate and fragmented.

By contrast, the chapters in this book accord a central place to changing directions in drug policies, not only in Britain but also in Europe. For that reason alone, it is to be welcomed. In addition, however, the chapters link their primary focus on drug use with aspects of gender, race, social exclusion and theory, all of which have a resonance in the current discourse of social policy. In doing so, they provide an important set of tools with which to rethink the diversity of drug use and drug users.

The chapters in this collection embody important theoretical and empirical perspectives. Their approach draws widely across the boundaries of academic disciplines. They ground policy changes in their substantive contexts and highlight the tensions that the drugs issue creates in the political arena. They provide evidence-based insights into the social complexities of both drug use and drug users. In all these ways, this book represents a contribution to the current political and policy debate. It also enables us to read behind the – often simplistic – headlines with greater understanding.

David Gladstone, University of Bristol

List of Abbreviations

ACMD	Advisory Council on the Misuse of Drugs
AIDS	Acquired immunodeficiency syndrome
ARS	Arrest Referral Schemes
ASRO	Addressing Substance Related Offending
BDWF	Black Drug Workers' Forum
CAD	Communities Against Drugs
CARAT	Counselling, Assessment, Referral, Advice and Throughcare
CDRP	Crime and Disorder Reduction Partnerships
CFI	Central Funding Initiative
CJIP	Criminal Justice Interventions Programme
CPS	Crown Prosecution Service
CRE	Commission for Racial Equality
DAT	Drug Action Teams
DDAC	District Drugs Advisory Committee
DDC	Drugs dependency clinic
DDU	Drug Dependency Units
DfES	Department for Education and Skills
DH	Department of Health
DHSS	Department of Health and Social Security
DIP	Drug Interventions Programme
DORIS	Drug Outcome Research in Scotland
DPAS	Drug Prevention Advisory Service
DRR	Drug Rehabilitation Requirement
DSD	Drugs Strategy Directorate
DTTO	Drug Treatment and Testing Orders
EMCDDA	European Monitoring Centre for Drugs and Drug Addiction
HIV	Human immunodeficiency virus

HMSO	Her Majesty's Stationery Office
ISDD	Institute for the Study of Drug Dependence
JCG	Joint Commission Group
LSD	Lysergic acid diethylamide
LSP	Local Strategic Partnerships
MDT	Mandatory drug testing
NDC	New Deal for Communities
NDS	National Drug Strategy
NEW-ADAM	New English and Welsh Drug Abuse Monitoring
NFF	New Futures Fund
NHS	National Health Service
NICE	National Institute for Clinical Excellence
NOMS	National Offender Management Service
NRU	Neighbourhood Renewal Unit
NSF	National Service Framework
NSNR	National Strategy for Neighbourhood Renewal
NTA	National Treatment Agency for Substance Misuse
NTORS	National Treatment Outcome Research Study
ODPM	Office of the Deputy Prime Minister
OSAP	Offender Substance Abuse Drug Interventions Programme
PCT	Primary Care Trust
QuADS	Quality Standards in Alcohol and Drugs Service
RDAC	Regional Drugs Advisory Committee
RDMD	Regional Drug Misuse Databases
RRA	Race Relations Act
RRAA	Race Relations Amendment Act
SCI	Safer Communities Initiative Fund
SCODA	Standing Conference on Drug Abuse
SEU	Social Exclusion Unit
SHHD	Scottish Home and Health Department
SRB	Single Regeneration Budget
SSD	Social services department
UKADCU	United Kingdom Anti-Drugs Coordination Unit
YOI	Young Offender Institutes

Editors' Introduction

Informed by both teaching and research, this volume is intended to resonate with a broad undergraduate and postgraduate audience interested in social policy and drugs. In designing the volume we thought it most appropriate that drug policy discussions were included within the context of a number of topical substantive themes, including social exclusion, gender, ethnicity, the law, criminal justice and health. A European perspective locates specific developments in the United Kingdom (UK), prior to a final chapter signalling how social theory can engage and augment understandings within the area of drugs policy. This reflects the way drugs as an issue have permeated all areas of social policy. It is impossible to discuss young people, criminal justice policy or social exclusion, for example, without acknowledging the role that drug use plays in those fields.

Some of our contributors allude to, and sometimes suggest in more explicit terms, that 'drugs are everyday'; rarely does a week pass without some high-level intervention into the ongoing development of drug policy in the UK. The drugs policy field is deeply politicised and discussion of policy must acknowledge the productive power of political expediency, or as Margaret Melrose suggests in Chapter 3, 'the politics of electoral anxiety'. The UK general election in 2005 was no exception with new Labour reporting that they would reconsider their decision to re-classify cannabis from Class B to Class C, within the context of research findings linking cannabis use to schizophrenia. However, by January 2006, perhaps somewhat surprisingly, the government had decided to retain the revised Class C categorization alongside the announcement that it was to embark on a publicity campaign to notify people of the potential risks. At the same time it announced that a 'wholesale review' of the way drugs were classified would be considered. Likewise, voices that call for the channelling of more resources into rehabilitative services, whilst scoring some modest success in recent years, remain peripheral to the central political thrust of the drugs debate – that of the continued 'war on drugs', or as Mike Shiner argues in Chapter 5, the drugs 'war zone'. It would seem that the enormity of the task to create 'drug free communities' (Her Majesty's Government 1998), for example, has almost overwhelmed a government, who like many before it, sense that the electorate is not yet ready for thinking the unthinkable in terms of radical reform in drugs policy. Yet, the unexpected contortions of the political scene have the power to constantly surprise. Perhaps we are approaching a policy crossroads that could usher in a more Europeanized model of tolerance towards drug users. However, like so much policy development in Britain, history suggests that we remain torn between the contrasting models and approaches characteristic of the United States on the one hand and elements of the European Union on the other.

In bringing together contributors for this volume we have included work that engages with empirical and theoretical concerns and, that as far as possible, captures current policy. In Chapter 1 Joanne Neale considers social exclusion which continues to be relatively unexplored within drugs policy. Neale's central argument is that 'where social exclusion and drugs appear together, only problematic drug use is ... considered' thereby neglecting recreational drug use. Inevitably, it is the problematic end of the drug taking spectrum that is invoked when the word drug is used. After tracing the heritage of social exclusion, Neale moves to highlight the links with drugs. Here, 'compounds' of personal and social conditions are noted to shape people's use of drugs. The social problems associated with community deprivation, unemployment, homelessness, poor health and crime, are considered prior to reflections on the ways in which social exclusion policies – both tangentially and in a more explicit sense – seek to alleviate vulnerability and disadvantage. Neale concludes the opening chapter by signalling social exclusion's ideological resonance that serves to obfuscate the fluidity and dynamism of individual's everyday experiences. In sum, she suggests that the complexity of problematic drug use (whether or not it involves 'included' or 'excluded' individuals) is not easily reconcilable with the politicised deployment of the term social exclusion.

Chapter 2, by Trish Harding, seeks to foreground the needs and circumstance of women in drugs policy and literature as a corrective to the decades-old, frequently implicit focus on men. This feminist inspired contribution highlight a number of challenges faced by women attempting to access drugs services. Harding argues how the norms and expectations that suffuse feminine or masculine continue to shape thinking in the field. In these terms, women are frequently understood to be 'doubly deviant' in that their drug use can be perceived to 'spoil their identities as mothers and carers'. Harding makes the important point that it is clear that women – as much as men – are very much active in a *non-victim* capacity in eclectic cultures of drug use. In conclusion, the chapter highlights the importance of developing gender sensitive policy in respect of strategy, the structures that shape women's opportunities and those of empowerment. Here, Harding stresses the importance of inter-agency working, the role of poverty, and approaches that respect, rather than condemn women problem drug users. Overall, whilst the message to emerge from this chapter is focused on women as a specific group, its resonance could be seen more broadly in signalling the importance of diversity to both theorising and policy.

Margaret Melrose focuses on young people and drugs in Chapter 3. She notes that young people and drugs are closely linked in the popular imagination as well as in policy discourse. Melrose's main proposition is that drug policy designed with this group in mind 'cannot be understood in isolation from developments in other policy areas'. Her discussion opens with an exploration of the socially constructed nature of the concepts of 'youth' and 'drugs'. In so doing, she demonstrates the historical, cultural and ideological forces shaping the conflation of these terms as a way to challenge the implicitly essentialist assumptions informing policy thinking. Echoing the analyses of other contributors to the volume, Melrose argues that it is socially excluded young people in particular that 'have been "othered" as a result of their position on the margins'. It is noted that this disadvantaged group have been identified by policy makers as the biggest threat to society.

Kazim Khan highlights a degree of convergence with 'problem youth' through his discussion of the ways in which racialised drug users are 'othered' in Chapter 4. That the terms 'race' and 'drugs' are closely intertwined through condemnatory discourses also mirrors those framing women in respect of their 'double deviance' In attempting to make sense of some of the recent policy developments in the drugs field with regard to race and ethnicity, Khan draws on the term 'ad-hocism'. Here, he argues that policies have tended to be driven by political rhetoric (for example, 'multiculturalism' and 'diversity'), rather than by challenging institutional prejudice. Khan adopts an activist stance in his writing, voicing strong views about drug users considered through their racial or ethnic identities. For example, he argues with some force that 'Doing something about it [racism] depends on tackling standard, taken for granted practices which are discriminatory in effect if not in intention'. The obstacles to progress are, he suggests, constituted by a paucity of knowledge around the drugs-race issue, together with the lack of responsibility demonstrated by a number of senior professionals involved in both drugs policy and practice.

In Chapter 5, 'Drugs, Law and the Regulation of Harm', Mike Shiner tackles the moral debate concerning the legal control of drugs. In sketching the legislative trajectory of drug policy, starting with a brief overview of 19th Century UK policy, he analyses the contradictions and tensions shaping the broad political consensus on prohibition that remains in the contemporary period. Shiner poses two key questions in relation to prohibition. 'What should be done?' and 'What can be done?'. He follows these with a discussion of the concept of harm in drug classification, use of the retributivist approaches in punishing users and suppliers, and the philosophical under-pinning of policy, conceived of in terms of utilitarianism. Shiner then goes on to introduce the findings of the Police Foundation's report that called for, amongst other things, a rethink of current drug classification. Rather than present a 'mirroring' exercise in which the harms of drugs might be com-prehensively downplayed, (frequently accompanying the call for the legal-isation of drugs; see Murji, 1998), Shiner draws attention to a way forward that would call for the 'reconfiguring of harm and the law'. The mechanism by which this might be achieved is restorative justice that, he argues, could be used to fuse care and control. The chapter ends with the argument that prohibition has failed, though politically it has been a 'spectacular' success. On a final optimistic note, there is acknowledgement that the ideological ground of drug policy might be shifting, flagged by the recent discussion of the value of harm reduction over that of retribution by the House of Commons Select Committee on Home Affairs (2002).

In Chapter 6, Rhidian Hughes and Nerys Anthony discuss the links between drugs and crime. They identify 'tensions within criminal justice policies, and between criminal justice and welfare policies.' Their point of entry into the chapter is to elucidate the synonymous nature – at least in the minds of politicians and policy makers – of drugs and crime. Reiterating the understanding of other contributors to this volume, they stress the difficulties of understanding drugs and crime as causally linked, and instead argue that this complex relationship should be placed within a broader social context. Hughes and Anthony make the important distinction between problem and recreational users, with the latter group moving into the criminal justice net in terms of the so-called policing of 'dinner party' cocaine users. Next, they warn against a conflation of lower end users with crime, developing an important theme of this volume – that of the diversity of drug users and drug use. Prior to a discussion of policy tensions in respect of the political context of debate through the 1980s and 1990s, they highlight the conceptual difficulties of unpacking the drugs and crime link. The authors' substantive discussion of Drug Treatment and Testing Orders (DTTO)/Drug Rehabilitation Requirement (DRR) demonstrates the many flaws inherent in 'the system'. One of a number, of these concerns is the ways in which there may exist a perverse incentive to secure a place on a DTTO/DRR to 'fast-track' into treatment. Hughes and Anthony return to the importance of locating users in their broader social contexts with drug treatment being noted to 'provide a criminal justice function'. Implicit in this chapter is the idea that the very status of illegal drugs may represent a vehicle on which the social control of the poor and disadvantaged can be credibly exercised.

Rachel Lart's chapter explores the way drugs policy can be seen to mirror broader concerns and directions in health policy. While acknowledging that health policy around drugs needs to be understood within the overall framework of legislative control and Home Office surveillance, she discusses how, at different periods, the medical/health contribution to the social response to drug use has been embedded in the prevailing norms and structures of health policy. Key themes explored in Lart's chapter include: the relationship between the medical profession and the state, the development of coordinating structures across sectors and between levels of government, and the growing significance of evidence based knowledge as a basis for policy. While Lart provides a historical summary, pointing to a broader literature on UK drugs policy, the period focused on is the last twenty years. Following Stimson (2000) she argues that these two decades have seen policy make a swing between a health oriented approach and a criminal justice one that has been perhaps more extreme than at any previous historical period.

In chapter 8 dealing with European drug policy, Henri Bergeron and Paul Griffiths provide a historical sketch of the patterns of convergence and divergence in drug policy at the European level. The three key substantive points discussed in their chapter are that first, until recently the idea of a 'common' European drug policy functioned at the level of rhetoric rather than reality. Second, that unlike policy developments in other fields across the Union, European drug policy is shaped by its diversity rather than homogeneity, an issue that is brought into particularly sharp focus when we consider the recent accession of a number of countries from eastern Europe. Finally, that despite the continuing differences in drug policies across Europe, they suggest that 'a drift towards convergence' might be occurring. Here, the continuing concern about the human immunodeficiency virus (HIV), and emerging concerns around the nexus linking public security with criminal activities and drugs, are now pushing their way up the European drugs' policy agenda. In the final chapter, Paul Higate discusses social theory within the context of drug taking. He argues that social theory that takes the embodiment of human agency, together with the socially productive forces of space and place, represent helpful theoretical paradigms with which to make sense of drug use and drug users. Fresh theoretical insight is particularly important when we consider the rapidly evolving social context of drug use. In distilling an emerging literature, Higate sketches some of the ways in which these theoretical insights have been applied in the drugs field. He brings chapter 9 to a close by arguing that the concepts of embodiment, space and place are useful tools with which to (re)think some of the social complexities of drug use and drug users.

Overall, this volume represents a modest attempt to consolidate and develop discussion and debate in the drugs policy field. Our intention has been to design a readily accessible map – in the form of an edited volume – to chart a number of the key aspects of this sphere of social policy. It is hoped that by grounding policy developments in their substantive contexts, readers will appreciate both the political and practical complexities that give rise to the character and effect of contemporary drug policy.

References

Her Majesty's (HM) Government (1998) *Tackling Drugs to Build a Better Britain: the Government's Ten Year Strategy for Tackling Drug Misuse.* London: Stationery Office.

Murji, K. (1998) 'The Agony and the Ecstasy: Drugs, Media and Morality' in R. Coomber (ed.) *The Control of Drugs and Drug Users.* Amsterdam: Harwood Academic Publishers.

Stimson, G.V. (2000) " 'Blair declares war': the unhealthy state of British drug policy" *International Journal of Drug Policy,* 11: 259–264.

chapter

one

Social Exclusion, Drugs and Policy

Joanne Neale

Introduction

In recent years, 'social exclusion' has become a widely used concept both nationally and internationally. Despite this, its meaning has been a matter of considerable debate (Room 1995; Levitas 1998; Percy-Smith 2000; Hills *et al.* 2002). Some would argue it is too simplistic or too political or too focused on paid work to be the platform for effective policy-making. Others would contend that it helpfully encapsulates the wide range of interacting and mutually reinforcing problems that individuals can sometimes face. Although problem drug users and drug misuse frequently feature in academic writings, policy documents and practice responses to social exclusion, there has been surprisingly little work directly linking these issues together. This chapter seeks to address this information gap by providing a critical reflection on how the concept of social exclusion has been, and currently is being, used in relation to drug misuse.

In order to undertake this, it is first necessary to point out that where social exclusion and drugs appear together, only problematic drug use is usually considered. For example, social exclusion is not likely to be invoked as an explanation for university students smoking cannabis; clubbers using ecstasy at the weekend; sports people taking performance-enhancing drugs; or city executives and media personalities snorting lines of cocaine. The most obvious explanation for this is that non-problematic users of drugs are often relatively affluent young people who are well integrated within key societal structures, such as the family, education, employment and housing. As such, debates about social exclusion do not easily fit their circumstances. This chapter also focuses on problematic drug use. It begins by considering the origins and definitions of social exclusion, before exploring links between its various dimensions and problematic drug use. Following this, policy responses to social exclusion that address drug misuse are examined and some strengths and weaknesses of using the concept to explain and respond to drug problems are suggested.

Origins and definitions of social exclusion

The term 'social exclusion' originated in France during the early 1970s. Initially, it was used to describe a relatively small number of social groups, such as people with learning difficulties or physical health problems; lone parents; substance users; and other people unprotected by social insurance. During the 1980s, however, the term spread to a much wider range of socially disadvantaged individuals and became central to French debates about the 'new poverty'. This 'new poverty' was the result of rapid economic transformations that had brought increased unemployment; growing family instability; a rise in single-person households; and a decline in class solidarity (MacPherson 1997; Smith 1999; Percy-Smith 2000).

Across Europe, social exclusion became popularized in the 1990s. For example, it was written into the Maastricht Treaty and became an object-ive for European structural funds (Room 1995). In the UK, it came to public attention in 1997 when New Labour established an interdepart-mental Social Exclusion Unit (SEU). As the concept of social exclusion has assumed greater political prominence at the European level, its meaning has tended to be adapted and modified to suit different political and national interpretations. So it has often been conflated with 'poverty' and/or 'exclusion from the labour market'. This has focused attention on economic deprivation and the need to link people back into paid employment, rather than on the broader economic, political, legal and social processes that can preclude people from full social participation (Smith 1999).

Despite these variations in usage and understanding, there is still a fairly general recognition that social exclusion is a multi-dimensional concept. It includes income poverty, but also encompasses inadequate social participa-tion lack of social integration and lack of power (Room 1995). Equally, it emphasizes the persistence of disadvantage over time and the concentration of social problems in particular geographical areas. Furthermore, it is con-cerned with the processes that underpin disadvantage. So, in addition to asking 'whether' people are socially excluded, it also raises questions about 'how' and 'why' that situation occurs. According to the Commission of the European Communities (1993: 3):

> Social exclusion refers to the multiple and changing factors resulting in people being excluded from the normal exchanges, practices and rights of modern society. Poverty is one of the most obvious factors, but

social exclusion also refers to inadequate rights in housing, education, health and access to services. It affects individuals and groups, particularly in urban and rural areas, who are in some way subject to discrimination or segregation; and it emphasizes the weaknesses in the social infrastructure and the risk of allowing a two-tier society to become established by default.

As Room (1995) argues, this definition has four particular strengths. First, it emphasizes the multiple factors associated with social exclusion (poverty, housing, health, education and access to services). Second, it refers to the dynamic nature of exclusionary processes (that is, the changing factors that disrupt normal exchanges). Third, it acknowledges societal responsibility for preventing the development of a two-tier society. And finally, it endorses the view that citizens within the European Union have rights to certain basic standards of living and to participation in key social and occupational institutions.

In the UK, the SEU has defined social exclusion slightly more narrowly as 'a shorthand label for what can happen when individuals or areas suffer from a combination of linked problems such as unemployment, poor skills, low incomes, poor housing, high crime environments, bad health and family breakdown' (SEU 1997: 1). This definition does not emphasize 'citizenship rights' or the 'processes' that can create social exclusion. However, it does recognize that the problem extends beyond low income and poverty and is compound and spatial in nature. Indeed, this appreciation of its complexity is confirmed in a recent SEU report that attributes the increase in social exclusion over recent years to rises in diverse but related problems, such as unemployment, the number of very disadvantaged people, children growing up in workless households, lone parents, crime, anti-social behaviour and drug misuse (SEU 2004).

Bradshaw *et al.* (2004) have similarly argued that social exclusion is driven by a range of factors, including demographic changes, labour market issues and public policies. Within this broad framework, they argue that problem drug use is a key dimension reflecting, causing and reinforcing social exclusion. Although also emphasizing that there is relatively little literature explicitly concerned with drugs and social exclusion, they nonetheless highlight that there is much research evidence on the relationship between drug use and various key indicators of social exclusion. Some of these links are explored below.

Linking drug use and social exclusion

Research has shown that problematic drug use (particularly among young people) is associated with a broad range of risk factors, including family disruption, poor relationships with parents, childhood abuse, school problems, childhood conduct disorder, crime, mental ill-health and social deprivation (Lloyd 1998). The links between these various risk factors are complex and it is not possible to say that any one causes another; simply that they are interrelated. Despite this, susceptibility to the various risks – and therefore to substance misuse – are more prevalent among particular subgroups of the population. These include homeless people, those who have been in local authority or foster care, pupils truanting or excluded from school, people who have been abused and those in contact with the criminal justice system or mental health services (Gilvarry 1998; Klee and Reid 1998; Powis *et al.* 1998).

Such complex interrelationships provide clear support for the compound nature of social problems, as highlighted in social exclusion debates. Meanwhile, a more detailed examination of exactly how the taking of illicit substances affects, or is affected by, particular dimensions of social exclusion provides further evidence of the links between these two phenomena. While it would be possible to investigate any of a long list of social exclusion indicators (family problems, disrupted education, exclusion from civic participation, poor access to services etc.), this chapter examines community deprivation, unemployment, homelessness, poor health and crime. These five dimensions comprise some of the most important indicators of social exclusion and collectively illustrate strong links with drug misuse.

Community deprivation

The association between drug use and community deprivation has been widely documented (Pearson *et al.* 1986; Advisory Council on the Misuse of Drugs (ACMD) 1998; Parker *et al.* 1998; Foster 2000). However, the precise nature of that relationship remains unclear. A recent government report (Drugs Strategy Directorate (DSD) 2002) states that drug problems are more likely to take root in deprived neighbourhoods for a number of reasons. For example, local people often feel cut off and powerless and their energy to tackle problems is likely to be eroded; people in deprived communities can often earn more money from selling illegal drugs than they can from any other legal means; there can be a concentration of residents with psychological and personal problems, for whom drugs may seem like an immediate solution; and impressionable young people may admire the violence, aggression and law-breaking associated with drug users and dealers.

At the same time, high levels of drug misuse can have particularly devastating consequences for poor local areas. This is because drugs fuel the burglary, robbery and anti-social behaviour that leaves many vulnerable people frightened to leave their homes (DSD 2001). The presence of drugs in a neighbourhood conveys a message to the inhabitants that the area is unsafe, fear is heightened and a downward spiral of crime, fear of crime and neighbourhood deterioration can be triggered (Wilson and Kelling 1982; Skogan 1990; Davis and Lurigio 1996). In short, neighbourhood disorganization may provide the opportunity for drug markets to become established while the existence of drug markets in a particular area may simultaneously precipitate other forms of social and community breakdown.

Unemployment

Research has regularly shown that problem drug users experience high levels of unemployment. For example, data from the British Crime Survey reveal a highly significant, negative statistical relationship between hard drug use and unemployment. In other words, people using hard drugs (such as heroin and cocaine) are much more likely to be unemployed than those who are not (MacDonald and Pudney 2000). A national longitudinal study of drug users beginning a new episode of drug treatment in Scotland also identified very high levels of labour market inactivity. Of 559 individuals recruited from community services, only 4 per cent were in paid employment at the time of their interview and only 13 per cent had been in legal paid employment at any point in the previous six months. The majority reported that their usual employment status over the previous three years had been unemployed or economically inactive (Kemp and Neale 2005).

Various reasons may account for the associations between problem drug use and unemployment. These include lifestyle, personal, health and other factors. For example, the constant need to acquire and use drugs can be incompatible with keeping regular working hours; both drug intoxication and withdrawal symptoms can have serious effects on work performance; and even daily visits to a pharmacy to collect prescribed medication (such as methadone) can disrupt the working day. A further barrier to employment encountered by both current and ex-drug users is discrimination from employers. This may occur either because employers are wary about taking on people with a known history of drug use (believing that they might be unreliable or untrustworthy) and/or because many drug users have a past criminal record. Finally, both the absence of secure housing and poor health (see below) can also hinder attempts to secure and maintain regular paid work.

Homelessness

Homelessness and drug problems are also very closely related. A study of 1000 predominantly young homeless people in hostels, day centres and on the streets of London found that 88 per cent were taking at least one drug and 35 per cent were heroin users (Flemen 1997). Similarly, Downing-Orr (1996) reported that 85 per cent of homeless youth in London and 83 per cent of homeless youth in Sydney were using illicit substances. In Scotland, a qualitative study of 200 drug users found that 136 respondents (68 per cent) had been homeless at some point in their lives and 63 (32 per cent) were homeless at the time of their interview (Neale 2002).

For some people, drug misuse is a key factor in becoming homeless. For others, the experience of homelessness induces drug misuse or exacerbates an existing drug problem. Equally, homelessness and addiction combined can reinforce each other and cause and/or intensify other related difficulties (Hutson and Liddiard 1994; Neale 2002). In consequence, homeless people who use drugs often experience multiple and interrelated problems, as a result of which they may require a broad range of support. As well as shelter and drug services, this can include practical assistance, health care, social and emotional support, financial or legal advice, and access to education, training and employment (Reid and Klee 1999; Fitzpatrick and Kennedy 2000).

Poor health

Drug addiction is thought to be directly responsible for some 3000 deaths a year. Moreover, roughly one in six of those who die – about 450 individuals – are under 25 years of age (DSD 2001). Intravenous injection is associated with human immunodeficiency virus (HIV), hepatitis infection, collapsed veins, septicaemia, bacterial infections, abscesses, endocarditis, arthritis and other rheumatologic complaints. Additionally, those with drug problems report a wide range of less dramatic, more mundane health problems, such as malnutrition, sleeping problems, tooth decay and loss of general levels of fitness (Neale 2002). The incidence of co-morbid psychiatric problems (including suicidality) among drug users is also widespread, although explanations for this remain unclear (Klee 1995; Neale 2000).

Poor health is, of course, associated with social exclusion in a variety of ways. For example, drug-related health problems can result in unemployment, limited social activities and reduced contact with family and friends. Meanwhile, social exclusion can result in unhealthy behaviour. Thus, those who are unemployed, homeless or socially isolated may be more inclined to take drugs to dull the boredom, isolation and monotony present in their lives. In particular, drug misuse is a major health problem within prisons. Among prisoners, the use of non-sterile injecting equipment is especially prevalent and this heightens the risks of both hepatitis and HIV infection. Equally, drug users recently discharged from prison are at increased risk of accidental overdose because of the greater availability of drugs outside the prison and their reduced tolerance while inside (Bradshaw *et al.* 2004).

Crime

Finally, the relationship between crime and drugs is examined. Although there is no conclusive evidence of a causal link between drug use and criminality, it is widely agreed that addiction to hard drugs is the cause of a significant amount of acquisitive crime (Seddon 2000); prolonged and regular polydrug use is associated with increased levels of offending (Bennett 1998, 2000); and the combination drug use and criminal behaviour can increase the risk of developing substance dependence and/or becoming a persistent offender (Hammersely *et al.* 2003). Perhaps unsurprisingly then, arrested individuals who use drugs have higher levels of self-reported crime than arrested non-drug users (Bennett 2000). Meanwhile, nearly three quarters (71 per cent) of the drug users participating in the English National Treatment Outcome Research Study (NTORS) reported that they had been arrested in the previous two years (Gossop *et al.* 1998).

It is estimated that nearly two thirds of persistent offenders are hard drug users and nearly three quarters started offending when they were between 13 and 15 years old. More than a third were in care as children, nearly half were excluded from school, half have no qualifications and very few have ever had a legitimate job (DSD 2001). A study of young people moving into adulthood in a disadvantaged neighbourhood in Teesside similarly found that young people with criminal careers shared a range of characteristics. These included disengagement from school by the age of 12 or 13, participation in street drinking with peers, drug use and petty crime from an early age and – in later life – progression to more serious crime and drug-taking (Johnston *et al.* 2000).

Tackling drug misuse through social exclusion policies

So far, this chapter has shown that there are strong associations between drug misuse and various key dimensions or indicators of social exclusion. The nature and direction of these relationships are often unclear but their existence and impact are nonetheless real. This section examines how policies designed to address social exclusion are impacting on drug use in the UK. It begins with an overview of the main organizations and bodies established by New Labour to help reintegrate excluded individuals and communities back into mainstream society. Thereafter, a number of social exclusion policies and initiatives that have particularly sought to address drug-related problems are considered.

Organizations and bodies

In 1997, New Labour set up the SEU to produce 'joined-up solutions to joined-up problems'. The overall aim was to 'develop integrated and sustainable approaches to the problems of the worst housing estates, including crime, drugs, unemployment, community breakdown, and bad schools etc.' (SEU 1997: 2). Since its inception, the Unit has produced reports and recommendations covering many exclusion-related topics, such as education for children in care, transport, young runaways, reoffending by ex-prisoners, neighbourhood renewal, opportunities for 16–18-year-olds not in education, employment or training, truancy and school exclusion, rough sleeping and teenage pregnancy. Although none of these reports has explicitly focused on drug users, those who take drugs feature among the various groups that have been considered.

In addition to establishing the SEU, the government set up new Whitehall units for neighbourhood renewal, rough sleepers, teenage pregnancy, and children and young people. It also created 18 new cross-departmental Policy Action Teams whose work falls under five broad themes: getting people into work; improving neighbourhoods and housing management; building a future for young people; ensuring access to services in the poorest areas; and improving the way government at all levels responds to social exclusion. The work of these diverse organizations and bodies has collectively contributed to important policy changes, new funding programmes and the setting of some tough new priorities and targets. Again, the drug problem has generally not appeared as a priority issue in its own right, but drug misuse is included in many of these broader developments and strategies.

Communities and neighbourhood renewal

In 1994, the Single Regeneration Budget (SRB) was introduced to simplify and streamline the assistance available for regeneration in England. Although the SRB predated New Labour, it had a clear social exclusion agenda and was an important source of funding for many community-led responses to drug use. Its key objective was to enhance the quality of life of local people living in areas of need by reducing the gap between deprived regions and other regions and between different groups. Under the SRB, local organizations were encouraged to bid for funding that would, for example, improve the education, skills and employment prospects of local people; generate opportunities for those who were disadvantaged; promote sustainable regeneration; support growth in local economies and businesses; increase community safety; and reduce crime and drug abuse.

Initiatives that were funded by the SRB had a diverse range of drug-related aims, including reducing the number of young people starting to use drugs (Normanton Regeneration); increasing the number of people accessing services (The People of Accrington and Church Together, Hyndburn); enabling ex-drug users to return to work (Safe in Tees Valley); reducing drug-related crime (Rural Tourism Development Area Partnership, West Lindsey); integrating drug services (Safe in Tees Valley); and increasing parental awareness of drugs (Wonford Regeneration Partnership, Exeter). In 2001, however, the SRB was superseded by the New Deal for Communities (NDC) programme, which thereafter became the main source of funding for local area regeneration in England and Wales.

The NDC is supported by the Neighbourhood Renewal Unit (NRU) but administered on a regional basis. Consistent with the aims of the SRB, it is mandated to narrow the gap between deprived communities and the rest of the country. Key differences between the NDC and previous regeneration programmes are the higher levels of funding available, the longer timeframes and the involvement of community residents in decision-making processes (National Audit Office 2004). As part of the NDC, the DSD has funded a long-term action research study of how drugs can be tackled in the most deprived communities. This has involved areas being allocated a neighbourhood drugs worker who is accountable to local residents and tasked with ensuring that their plans are effectively implemented (Drugs Strategy Directorate 2004a).

Box 1.1

New Deal for Communities (NDC) Practice Example: West Middlesborough
This partnership has a budget for tackling drug problems in their area and has developed plans for building local treatment, involving local people, providing diversionary activity, training and after-care for ex-prisoners, and action on supply. The Home Office DSD has assisted this partnership via a research programme to enhance its development of drug issues. This has involved employing a local drugs coordinator who is accountable to local residents involved in the NDC board. Through funding and a dedicated staff member, the activity on drugs within the area is accountable to local people; is focused and led by one individual; and ensures accountability to the funding sources in government office (Drug Strategy Directorate 2002: 22)

In addition to the NDC, the government has supported regeneration in 88 of the most deprived local authority districts with an extensive Neighbourhood Renewal Fund (NRF). This is being administered by Local Strategic Partnerships (LSPs) – single bodies that bring together all the key players in a local area, including the different parts of the public, private, voluntary and community sectors. NRF money can be spent by the participating neighbourhoods in any way that they believe will tackle deprivation, including that caused by local drug problems. LSPs are increasingly working with Drug Action Teams (DATs) to explore how aspects of the law (such as that on closing premises used for drug supply and speeding up processes for obtaining possession orders) can be adapted to improve regeneration practice. Also, they are working together to provide comprehensive guidance on issues such as housing management, clubs, begging, sex markets, homelessness and drugs in the workplace (ODPM 2005).

Further to the above, the government has developed the 'Positive Futures' programme (a national sports and arts-based social inclusion programme) to help young people withstand the pressure of becoming involved in substance use and offending (DSD 2001). Additionally, money has been made available to encourage partnership working in tackling the related problems of drugs and crime. For example, the Communities Against Drugs (CAD) strategy was established to empower and mobilize local communities to respond to their own drug problems and drug-related crime. This was achieved by giving DATs and Crime and Disorder Reduction Partnerships (CDRPs) resources so that they could build stronger community links and help the police and local people tackle neighbourhood problems together.

Decisions about how CAD money was to be spent were made locally by involving schools, parents, the police, voluntary organizations, local government, health professionals and local businesses. A wide range of initiatives could be funded, such as neighbourhood wardens to provide a constant presence on housing estates and other public areas; action to tackle drug-related anti-social behaviour, for example through Anti-Social Behaviour Orders; more and better anti-drugs education in schools; action to tackle truancy and school exclusions; support for community, parents' and residents' groups; close circuit television, better security lighting, and physical changes (such as gates and blocking off alleyways) to improve feelings of public safety; and targeted measures to tackle drug-related crimes such as burglary, theft and robbery (DSD 2001).

After April 2003, funding for CAD was combined with the Partnership Development Fund (PDF) to form a single funding stream, the Building Safer Communities (BSC) Fund. The BSC Fund is a three-year programme designed to enable CDRPs and DATs to achieve better outcomes by taking a more holistic and structured approach to reducing crime and other drug-related problems. BSC funding is to be used in a similar way to CAD money to support a diverse range of local initiatives, such as housing work to manage drug problems; tackling anti-social behaviour related to drugs, including begging or prostitution; developing parents' and residents' groups; work with homeless drug users; needle collection or awareness campaigns; community development work, including education, awareness and patch-based drugs workers; and action to tackle drug supply.

Drug treatment services

Although the government has not placed the provision of drug treatment services at the centre of its response to social exclusion, the importance of drug treatment in tackling aspects of social exclusion, particularly community deprivation and crime, has been recognized. For example, guidance on the commissioning of drug services has been developed so that the multiple and varying needs of problem drug users can be better addressed. In addition, an action plan to reduce drug-related deaths was published in 2001 and, during the same year, the National Treatment Agency (NTA) was established. The NTA's aim is to double the number of people in effective, well-managed treatment in England from 100,000 in 1998 to 200,000 in 2008 and to work with a wide range of agencies (such as housing organizations, higher education establishments and employers) to ensure that recovering drug users have opportunities to rebuild their lives and contribute usefully to their communities (DSD 2004b).

Complementing this, increasing investment is being made in engaging drug misusing offenders in treatment via arrest referral schemes that pick up drug users at the point of arrest and refer them into treatment or other programmes of help; drug testing in police custody to better inform bail and sentencing decisions; Drug Treatment and Testing Orders (DTTOs) to enable offenders to address their problem through intensive community-based programmes; expanding treatment provision in prisons; and improved through-care and after care links for prisoners returning to the community. Potentially, these measures enable people who are financing their drug use through crime to be identified and assisted at a much earlier stage than previously. Equally, the aim is to provide a complete package of care for people experiencing drug problems in order to give them every chance of moving out of the downward spiral that can be triggered by addiction (DSD 2001).

Employment

Consistent with the emphasis on paid work within social exclusion rhetoric, New Labour has developed a range of programmes to increase the employability of individuals who are long-term unemployed or economically inactive. One of the most important of these has been the New Deal (for example, the New Deal for Young People, the New Deal 25 Plus, and the New Deal for Lone Parents). Research has, however, found that New Deal programmes have been most useful in helping individuals who are more or less job ready. In contrast, people who experience multiple disadvantages and have complex needs – such as problem drug users, homeless people and ex-offenders – often require more intensive, specialized forms of support before they can contemplate paid work (Social Security Advisory Committee

2002; SEU 2004). In recognition of this, New Labour introduced a new – albeit much smaller – initiative called 'Progress2work' in 2001. This scheme seeks to help people who have either completed a drug treatment programme or who are undergoing treatment and have a dependence that is stabilized. In Scotland, meanwhile, the Scottish Executive introduced the New Futures Fund (NFF). This aims to reduce social exclusion and disadvantage by funding projects to help vulnerable groups of young people (including drug users) move closer to work.

Box 1.2

NFF Practice Example: East End Partnership, Glasgow. This project will work with clients aged 16–34 to develop confidence, core skills, communication, timekeeping, teamwork, literacy and numeracy via one-to-one and group work. The project will integrate with the existing drugs employment worker currently in place who will then support clients into employment/training (Scottish Enterprise 2003:9).

Children and young people

On a more general level, the government has been addressing social exclusion by investing money in tackling truancy and school exclusion and by developing policies to improve the life chances of children in care. To this end, a new Children's Fund was established to help identify children and young people who are showing early signs of disturbance and to provide them and their families with the support they need to re-establish some stability in their lives. Additionally, money has been available from the Children and Young Person's Unit for projects testing out innovative ways of working with runaways, providing evidence of what works best, and informing the future planning of runaway services (SEU 2002). Together, these measures engage with, and seek to tackle, some of the underlying reasons why young people can find themselves drifting into drug use.

Some concluding comments

This chapter began by documenting the increasing popularity and usage of the term 'social exclusion'. It also showed how definitions of the concept have varied, but generally recognize the multi-dimensional nature of difficulties, the persistence of disadvantage over time, and the concentration of social problems in particular places. Despite gaps in the existing literature and research, drug-taking is closely associated with many aspects of social exclusion and thus an important dimension of it. Accordingly, a number of recent policies and strategies designed to tackle social exclusion have – either directly or indirectly – brought new resources, new ideas and some new priorities into the drugs field. Of these, funding for CAD (now incorporated within the Building Safer Communities Fund), an expansion of drug treatment services and specialized employment programmes such as Progress2Work and the NFF are probably the most salient.

To what extent the various measures implemented under the broad banner of social exclusion will actually be successful in preventing and addressing drug problems is, however, a moot point. The report *Tackling Social Exclusion: Taking Stock and Looking to the Future. Emerging Findings*, published in 2004, concluded that progress in tackling social exclusion was being made, but much still needed to be done and people experiencing drug problems were one of the most difficult groups to reach (SEU 2004). Studies evaluating the effectiveness of the various social exclusion-related initiatives will no doubt proliferate over the next few years, but in the meantime it is only possible to speculate about whether the money and human resources being invested are generating maximum returns or whether alternative approaches could produce equal or better outcomes. In the absence of hard evidence, this chapter cannot provide any definitive answers. It does nonetheless seem prudent to conclude with a few words of caution.

As indicated in the Introduction, one of the most obvious limitations of using social exclusion to explain drug use is the concept's inability to account for both recreational forms of drug-taking and problematic use by individuals who are otherwise well-integrated members of society (e.g. middle-class professionals, athletes or people working in the music and entertainment industry). This does not deny the relevance, or indeed importance, of social exclusion as a key factor in the aetiology of much, if not most, drug misuse. However, it does mean that other explanations are required for other forms of drug-taking. A further difficulty, meanwhile, arises in relation to the lack of clarity often evident in definitions of social exclusion. Its conflation with both poverty and unemployment produces rather narrow conceptions that exclude individuals marginalized because of other life circumstances. Conversely, the breadth and diversity of problems encompassed by social exclusion can produce an equally unsatisfactory situation whereby everyone seems to be excluded on at least one dimension.

Lumping large numbers of people together and labelling them as socially excluded can cause as many problems as it solves. Clearly, many people live in deprived communities and/or are homeless and/or are long-term unemployed. Yet, many of these will never experiment with, let alone become dependent on, drugs. People's experiences of life problems (be this poverty or ill-health or addiction) are inevitably diverse and consequently require diverse solutions. Blanket categorizations can mask that diversity. Also, they can make people feel stigmatized and helpless. People who score highly on one or two dimensions of social exclusion can suddenly find themselves scoring highly on others. So, children who truant and behave badly may be labelled as drug users; unemployed youth who smoke cannabis can be stereotyped as hardened criminals; and whole communities can find themselves stigmatized simply because drug dealers operate near their homes. Living in a neighbourhood considered to have a high deprivation score might well bring in additional money through special neighbourhood funds and grants. Nonetheless, it may also deter employers from investing locally or may result in individuals with particular addresses or postcodes being turned down for work.

Finally, it is important to remember that drug misuse is one of the most pressing social issues facing society today. It wastes lives and human potential, destroys relationships and costs society huge amounts of money in terms of crimes committed, policing and punishment, treatment and general health care. It might then be argued that the most effective policies and strategies to tackle drug problems will be those that are driven by drug misuse *per se*, not those that are filtered through some other policy lens such as social exclusion. Similarly, the best people to inform us about availability, prevention, treatment and rehabilitation are those who are or who have been addicted, not those representing some other local interest group – for example, community safety or urban renewal. There is a danger that allowing a social exclusion agenda to determine our drug policies will skew services heavily towards those that attempt to prevent crime, reassure the frightened and promote employment – that is, away from those that prioritize the complex needs of people who are actually addicted.

To conclude, the concept of social exclusion offers both strengths and weaknesses in respect of explaining and responding to drug use. It can help us to understand some, but cannot account for all, forms of drug-taking. Drug misuse is a complicated phenomenon and to date no single theory has satisfactorily explained the many and various forms it can take. Diverse physiological, psychological and sociological analyses all form part of a broad spectrum of explanations and the concept of social exclusion certainly deserves a place alongside them. However, it does not offer a comprehensive and faultless alternative to their respective limitations. Similarly, in terms of policy and practice, the focus on social exclusion has generated new policies, priorities and funds and these should certainly complement and build upon what has already gone before. Despite this, it is important not to lose sight of the fact that initiatives primarily designed to address another complex (and often vague) agenda and another broad set of interests will in all likelihood provide less than optimal answers to a problem that is already known to be incredibly complicated and has no simple solution.

References

Advisory Council on the Misuse of Drugs (ACMD) (1998) *Drug Misuse and the Environment*. London: Stationery Office.

Bennett, T.H. (1998) *Drugs and Crime: The Results of Research on Drug Testing and Interviewing Arrestees*. Home Office Research Study 183. London: Home Office.

Bennett, T.H. (2000) *Drugs and Crime: The results of the Second Development Stage of the NEW-ADAM Programme*. Home Office Research Study 205. London: Home Office.

Bradshaw, J., Kemp, P., Baldwin, S. and Rowe, A. (2004) *The Drivers of Social Exclusion. A Review of the Literature*. York: Social Policy Research Unit, University of York.

Commission of the European Communities (1993) *Background Report: Social Exclusion – Poverty and Other Social Problems in the European Community*, ISEC/B11/93. Luxembourg: Office for the Publications of the European Communities.

Davis, R.C. and Lurigio, A.J. (1996) *Fighting Back: Neighborhood Antidrug Strategies*. London: Sage.

Downing-Orr, K. (1996) *Alienation and Social Support: A Social Psychological Study of Homeless Young People in London and in Sydney*. Aldershot: Avebury.

Drugs Strategy Directorate (DSD) (2001) *Communities Against Drugs*. London: Home Office.

Drugs Strategy Directorate (DSD) (2002) *Tackling Drugs as Part of Neighbourhood Renewal*. London: Home Office.

Drugs Strategy Directorate (DSD) (2004a) *Multi-component Programmes*. www.drugs.gov.uk/NationalStrategy/Communities/Toolkits/Community Development/Multi-componentprogrammes (accessed 9 March 2005).

Drugs Strategy Directorate (DSD) (2004b) *National Treatment Agency for Substance Misuse (NTA)*. www.drugs.gov.uk/NationalStrategy/Treatment/ NationalTreatmentAgency (accessed 9 March 2005).

Fitzpatrick, S. and Kennedy, C. (2000) *Getting By: Begging, Rough Sleeping and The Big Issue in Glasgow and Edinburgh*. Bristol: Policy Press.

Flemen, K. (1997) *Smoke and Whispers: Drugs and Youth Homelessness in Central London*. London: Turning Point/Hungerford Drug Project.

Foster, J. (2000) Social exclusion, crime and drugs, *Drugs: Education, Prevention and Policy*, 7: 317–30.

Gilvarry, E. (1998) Young drug users: early intervention, *Drugs: Education, Prevention and Policy*, 5: 281–92.

Gossop, M., Marsden, J. and Stewart, D. (1998) *NTORS at One Year: Changes in Substance Use, Health and Criminal Behaviour One Year After Intake*. London: Department of Health.

Hammersley, R., Marsland, L. and Reid, M. (2003) *Substance Use by Young Offenders*, Home Office Findings 172. London: Home Office.

Hills, J., Le Grand, J. and Piachaud, D. (eds) (2002) *Understanding Social Exclusion*. Oxford: Oxford University Press.

Hutson, S. and Liddiard, M. (1994) *Youth Homelessness*. London: Macmillan.

Johnston, L., MacDonald, R., Mason, P., Ridley, L. and Webster, C. (2000) *Snakes and Ladders: Young People, Transition and Social Exclusion*. Bristol: Policy Press/Joseph Rowntree Foundation.

Kemp, P.A. and Neale, J. (2005) Employability and problem drug users, *Critical Social Policy*, 25: 28–46.

Klee, H. (1995) Drug misuse and suicide: assessing the impact of HIV, *AIDS Care*, 7: 145–55.

Klee, H. and Reid, P. (1998) Drugs and youth homelessness: reducing the risk, *Drugs: Education, Prevention and Policy*, 5: 269–80.

Levitas, R. (1998) *The Inclusive Society*. Basingstoke: Macmillan.

Lloyd, C. (1998) Risk factors for problem drug use: Identifying vulnerable groups, *Drugs: Education, Prevention and Policy*, 5: 217–32.

MacDonald, Z. and Pudney, S. (2000) Illicit drug use, unemployment, and occupational attainment, *Journal of Health Economics*, 19: 1089–15.

MacPherson, S. (1997) Social exclusion, *Journal of Social Policy*, 26: 533–41.

National Audit Office (2004) *An Early Progress Report on the New Deal for Communities Programme*. London: Stationery Office.

Neale, J. (2000) Suicidal intent in non-fatal illicit drug overdose, *Addiction*, 95: 85–93.

Neale, J. (2002) *Drug Users in Society*. Basingstoke: Palgrave.

ODPM (Office of the Deputy Prime Minister) (2005) *Drug Abuse*. www.neighbourhood.gov.uk/page.asp?id=684 (accessed 9 March 2005).

Parker, H., Bury, C. and Eggington, R. (1998) *New Heroin Outbreak Among Young People in England and Wales*, Police Research Group, Crime Prevention and Detection Series Paper 92. London: HMSO.

Pearson, G., Gilman, M. and McIver, S. (1986) *Young People and Heroin. An Examination of Heroin Use in the North of England*, Health Education Council Report 8. London: Health Education Council.

Percy-Smith, J. (ed.) (2000) *Policy Responses to Social Exclusion. Towards Inclusion?* Buckingham: Open University Press.

Powis, B., Griffiths, P., Gossop, M., Lloyd, C. and Strang, J. (1998) Drug use and offending behaviour among young people excluded from school, *Drugs: Education, Prevention and Policy*, 5: 245–56.

Reid, P. and Klee, H. (1999) Young homeless people and service provision, *Health and Social Care in the Community*, 7: 17–24.

Room, G. (ed.) (1995) *Beyond the Threshold: The Measurement and Analysis of Social Exclusion*, Bristol: Policy Press.

Scottish Enterprise (2003) *New Futures Fund: Phase Two*. Glasgow: Scottish Enterprise.

Seddon, T. (2000) Explaining the drug-crime link: theoretical, policy and research issues, *Journal of Social Policy*, 29: 95–107.

SEU (Social Exclusion Unit) (1997) *Social Exclusion Unit: Purpose, Work Priorities and Working Methods*. London: HMSO.

SEU (Social Exclusion Unit) (2002) *Young Runaways*. London: Office of the Deputy Prime Minister.

SEU (Social Exclusion Unit) (2004) *Tackling Social Exclusion: Taking Stock and Looking to the Future. Emerging Findings*. London: Office of the Deputy Prime Minister.

Skogan, W.G. (1990) *Disorder and Decline: Crime and the Spiral to Decay in American Cities.* New York: Free Press.

Smith, J. (1999) Youth homelessness in the UK: A European perspective, *Habitat International*, 23: 63–77.

Social Security Advisory Committee (2002) *Fifteenth Report April 2001–March 2002.* Leeds: Corporate Document Services.

Wilson, J.Q. and Kelling, G. (1982) Broken windows: the police and neighbourhood safety, *Atlantic Monthly*, 3: 29–36.

Further reading

Drugs Strategy Directorate (2001) *Communities Against Drugs.* London: Home Office.

Drugs Strategy Directorate (2002) *Tackling Drugs as Part of Neighbourhood Renewal.* London: Home Office.

Guardian Unlimited (2004) *Social Exclusion: Resources.* http://society.guardian.co.uk/socialexclusion/0,11499,630068,00.html (accessed 9 March 2005).

Hills, J., Le Grand, J. and Piachaud, D. (eds) (2002) *Understanding Social Exclusion.* Oxford: Oxford University Press.

London School of Economics (2004) *CASE Centre for Analysis of Social Exclusion.* http://sticerd.lse.ac.uk/case (accessed 9 March 2005).

Office of the Deputy Prime Minister (2004) *The Social Exclusion Unit.* www.socialexclusionunit.gov.uk (accessed 9 March 2005).

Percy-Smith, J. (ed.) (2000) *Policy Responses to Social Exclusion. Towards Inclusion?* Buckingham: Open University Press.

Social Exclusion Unit (2004) *Tackling Social Exclusion: Taking Stock and Looking to the Future. Emerging Findings.* London: Office of the Deputy Prime Minister.

chapter

two

Gender, Drugs and Policy

Trish Harding

Introduction

In 1989, the Advisory Council for the Misuse of Drugs (ACMD 1989) suggested drug services should review their policies to ensure services were receptive to women's needs. Although concerned with the significance of gender for drugs policy, the focus of this chapter is about women and illicit drug use. This focus reflects an emphasis on 'women' in the literature on gender, which has highlighted the predominance of a male perspective in research studies and the tendency to consider this as the 'norm' in terms of policy development. Writing in the early 1990s Taylor (1993: 1), for instance, noted that '[m]ost research in the field of illicit drug use has overwhelmingly concentrated on young male users, and females are either ignored or seen as marginal'. Barber (1995: 117–18) subsequently questioned the validity of service provision and treatment models for women drug users, stating that 'because women are so greatly underrepresented in addiction research and treatment, our existing methods have largely been developed by and for men'. A decade later, Ettore (2004) notes that the situation has changed little and despite a greater awareness of gender, there remain fewer studies of women than of men and drug use. There is an argument for continued focus on women but, as Henderson (1999) suggests, this should embrace an understanding of the different cultures of women's drug use rather than simply offer a 'one-size-fits-all approach'.

This chapter will consider the challenge for policy-makers in distinguishing the needs and circumstances of women drug users and the implications for policy responses. It will examine how the growing awareness of gender, or women's issues, within national drugs policy during the last two decades has been shaped by the ways women's drug use has been portrayed within drugs research and literature. Typically, women have been both viewed and represented as deviant, promiscuous or as passive victims, and on the whole, policy and service provision has reflected this view. However, in recent years this situation has changed and the emerging literature and theorizing concerning women's drug use is considered along with its potential impact on future policy trends.

Gender and current drugs policy

As a major plank of its ten-year national drug strategy, the government has been concerned to reduce the demand for drugs by reducing the number of problem drug users and increasing their participation in drug treatment programmes (HM Government 1998). The government's Updated Drug Strategy in 2002 heralded the Strategy's success in reaching its key performance targets in this respect. The government's summary referred to being 'on track to meet the target of doubling the number of people in treatment by 2008' (Home Office 2002: 11). However, there has been a growing recognition that the specific needs and experiences of women with problematic drug use, and the barriers these women face in accessing services, are not adequately being addressed within current policies and interventions. Reports published over the last decade have raised awareness of the need for gender-specific services, particularly for women drug users with children (Task Force 1996; ACMD 1998; European Monitoring Centre for Drugs and Drug Addiction (EMCDDA) 2000). The *United Kingdom Anti-Drugs Co-ordinator's Annual Report 2000–01* drew attention to the continuing tendency of drug services to focus on the needs of white male drug users and to be less concerned about the inadequacy of specific services for women and minority ethnic communities (Home Office 2001). The report stated that the UK Anti-Drugs Coordination Unit (UKADCU), in conjunction with the Drug Prevention Advisory Service (DPAS), had commissioned research to inform the development of improved services for women. The resulting report, *Women Drug Users and Drugs Service Provision* (Becker and Duffy 2002), shed light on why services find it difficult when engaging women and makes recommendations relating to policy and practice as well as identifying further research needs. The message was 'that women problem drug users have specific experiences and complex needs which are not always recognised or met' (p. 2). Drawing on existing literature, the authors identify four distinct issues faced by women problem drug users for services to take on board in developing better provision for women – pregnancy and childcare; sex-work; sexual and physical abuse; and mental health needs. The National Crack Action Plan published by the Home Office in 2002 highlights the strong association between crack use and sex work and intends to commission specialist treatment programmes for people most affected by crack, such as sex workers (Home Office 2002).

To facilitate a target of increased participation in treatment programmes, the Department of Health established the National Treatment Agency for Substance Misuse (NTA) in 2001 to oversee the expansion and delivery of treatment services in England. This was followed in 2002 by the publication of a national service framework for drug treatment – *Models of Care for the Treatment of Adult Drug Misusers* (NTA 2002). *Models of Care* was introduced to address the existing 'post-code lottery' to treatment by offering a structural framework for the commissioning and provision of drug services around the country, along with mechanisms to review and audit services against quality standards and an evidence base of good practice (NTA 2002). Within its discussion of the principles underpinning a four-tiered system for treatment services, the document requires commissioners to recognize gender and ethnicity and to ensure equal access to services. Becker and Duffy note the need to address major gaps in service provision for particular groups of women, including ethnic minority women, women with mental health problems and women in contact with the criminal justice system. They call on treatment commissioners to address these inequalities and propose that the NTA take a lead role in the development of services by setting up a 'national gender-specific advisory group with regional representation' (Becker and Duffy 2002: 42).

Becker and Duffy (2002: 16) also note that women drug users in prison 'appear to be a particularly needy group compared to the general population, to other prisoners and to drug dependent men in prison'. They refer to statistical patterns indicating that women imprisoned for drug offences have 'a high incidence of abuse and trauma, disrupted care during childhood, low levels of education, social isolation and a high prevalence of mental disorder' (2002: 16). Drug policy for women prisoners is administered under the *Prison Service Drugs Strategy* (HM Prison Service 1998). This strategy accompanied the launch of the ten-year national strategy and mirrors the aims of the former but within a prison context. Smyth (2000) points to a recognition within the strategy of the differing needs of women prison populations from the general prison population, and an awareness of the particular problem of providing adequate treatment for short-term and remand prisoners, many of whom were likely to be women. Knowledge on the effectiveness for women of new prison drug treatment initiatives[1] and that of community sentencing orders such as the Drug Treatment and Testing Order (DTTO) is still limited. Becker and Duffy (2002: key findings)

---

1 Alongside the development of CARAT services (Counselling, Assessment, Referral, Advice and Throughcare), the *Prison Service Drugs Strategy* anticipated that women prisoners would benefit from the planned expansion in detoxification facilities and from the number of rehabilitation programmes available within women's prisons. In a further policy document, *The Government's Strategy for Women Offenders*, the Home Office (2000) later expressed a commitment to evaluating the effectiveness of these services for women prisoners.

remark, however, that interventions within the criminal justice system 'have been more successful in attracting young, white male users than women'.

Any consideration here of drugs policy aimed specifically at addressing women's needs and circumstances has to be informed by a theoretical discussion of women's illicit drug use. In this discussion I wish first to develop an understanding of the concept of 'gender' in relation to drug use before moving on to examine some of the theories of women's drug use.

Understanding the concept of gender in relation to women's drug use

The literature on drug use has identified that while women and men problem drug users may face many of the same difficulties, as a result of their shared experience of addiction, there are major areas of difference in their circumstances and needs. As Wright (2002) points out, these differences relate to gender and mirror societal differences between women and men. One way of approaching an understanding of the significance of gender for drugs policy is to focus on these differences and their bearing on service provision. In doing so, it is important to recognize the heterogeneity of problem drug users. Hence gender differences will intersect with differences among users both in the nature of their drug use and in terms of ethnicity, culture, social class, age, sexual orientation, physical and mental ability (Stevens *et al.* 1998; Patel 2000). In an investigation of differences between men and women drug users seeking treatment as part of the Drug Outcome Research in Scotland (DORIS) study for instance, Beale (2004: 863) found 'a great diversity of individual experience among new clients suggesting that there is no "typical" men or "typical" women new treatment client'.

A further consideration is the way in which gender is perceived or measured within social science. Some writers have stressed a need to recognize that 'gender' is a socially constructed phenomenon. Within a feminist theoretical perspective, Ettore (1992) for example, points to the need to view women's drug use within the 'ideology of reproduction' and the 'ideology of femininity'. She argues that drugs cannot, therefore, be divorced from the social construction of women's role. In discussing the ways in which perceptions of women's drug use are linked with perceptions of femininity, Malloch (2000: 55) notes that in engaging in illicit drug use, a pursuit traditionally viewed as 'masculine', women problem drug users are seen as doubly deviant – not only engaging in law-breaking but also going 'against acceptable notions of femininity'. This is in contrast to a perceived compatibility between men's problem drug use and notions of masculinity. Campbell (2000: 215) points to the view that to a certain extent '[d]rug use in men is understood as a risk-taking behaviour that falls within culturally appropriate expressions of masculinity'. In Collison's (1996: 428) work on drugs and crime, for instance, he describes how for young males growing up in marginalized communities, drug consumption and dealing, and the risks attached to these activities, serve to produce 'a particular, and powerful, masculine identity on the street'. As well as being part of the local 'irregular' economy and offering material success, Collison found that drugs, and drug crime, offered a certain cultural role model for young men. However, as Henderson's (1999) study of recreational ecstasy use reveals, gender roles vary between drug cultures and notions of masculinity and femininity are constantly changing. For instance, evidence suggests that within the pleasure-seeking dance cultures of the 1990s, illicit drug use was viewed as an acceptable risk-taking behaviour for both women and men (Henderson 1999; Hutton 2004). That this has resulted in a narrowing of the traditional gender difference in drug use is not surprising. As Collison (1996: 433) remarks, 'these drugs (and their imagery) are not marketed in simply (masculine) gendered ways, nor in traditionally gendered places (on the street corner)'.

Ettore (1992) notes the socialization of women into dependency roles as particularly relevant to women's drug use. Within a framework of critical criminology, Malloch (2000) suggests that for women problem drug users, the question of whether or not their dependency is controlled within prevailing power relations is a significant one. If it is a form of dependency externally controlled by doctors, for instance, then it is socially acceptable. However, should women engage in drug use independently or illegally then it is considered hedonistic or deviant. Drawing upon the work of Perry (1991) and Ettore and Riska (1995), Malloch (2000) highlights a contradiction within women's problem drug use between the moral condemnation of illicit drug use and the social acceptability of medically prescribed drug use – a contradiction that rarely applies to men as, traditionally, men are less likely than women to be dependent on prescribed drugs. In their historical analysis of women's problem drug use, Straussner and Attia (2002) discuss its iatrogenic nature. They describe the extensive and long-term prescribing of opiates and cocaine to women in the USA during the nineteenth century and its contribution to the growth of the pharmaceutical industry at this time. They believe it is instructive to adopt a historical perspective as it both informs an understanding of women's problem drug use within the context of women's role in society and an understanding of policy responses.

In addition to observing the social definition of 'gender', we need to recognize also that 'drug misuse' is a socially constructed and changing phenomenon and, as McGregor (2000: 34) notes 'one which is imbued with moral questions'. For example, the focus on drugs and crime within the ten-year strategy suggested a shift in policy emphasis from one previously concerned with public health and harm reduction to one concerned with crime and crime reduction (Stimson 2000). A historical and political analysis of problem drug use shows that clearly it is interwoven with ideology and politics (Raven 2001). Ettore (1992) suggests there is a need for a theoretical perspective that views problem drug use as a complex historical and social issue with specific political implications.

Theories of women's drug use

Ettore's (1992) feminist analysis of women and drug use in the early 1990s calling for the recognition of 'gender' as a key concept in this field of study was part of a shift in focus away from a clinical or epidemiological bias towards perspectives that recognize the political, social and cultural forces shaping problem drug use. Other commentators, many of whom were influenced by feminist theory, have expanded upon this discourse. In her feminist critical policy analysis of women and drugs in the USA, Campbell (2000: 14) shows how women's problem drug use 'has been constructed as a gendered, racialized, and sexualized threat to modernity, capitalist production, social reproduction, and democratic citizenship'. Notably, Campbell (p. 3) shows the way in which differential drug use opportunities between white women and African-American women have been racialized – that is, white women's use of 'meth' or 'crank' and black women's use of crack cocaine. She suggests that white women's problem drug use has been characterized as somehow 'cleaner', more 'functional' and more 'orderly' than that of black crack-using women who are characterized as 'sexual compulsives', 'bad mothers' and 'willing prostitutes'.

The theory that women's problem drug use can have a basis in the multiple natures of women's social roles and in their status in society has been a recurring theme in the literature for many years. Henderson (1990) points to the way in which women's roles affect access to services. In an examination of drugs and human immunodeficiency virus (HIV) services for women she highlights, for example, the tendency of women to prioritize the welfare needs of others over their own and to find difficulty in accessing services for themselves. Within a feminist analysis, Sargent (1992) highlights the significance of power relations to women's drug use. Thus women's drug use can be placed within the same theoretical perspective as domestic violence or rape – as an extension or enforcement of men's power over women. Ettore (1992) suggests however that a feminist analysis should explore the question of whether women experience drug use as pleasurable and whether or not it can contribute to a woman's sense of well-being. She raises questions about women's drug use for sexual pleasure, for greater autonomy and also as a means of empowerment. Henderson (1999) has turned to cultural studies for an understanding of women's drug use for fun and pleasure. She suggests that for the young women in her study, ecstasy use could be viewed within the context of popular consumer culture. This allows for a perspective of women drug users as being 'social actors, rather than merely passive subjects of power' (Henderson 1999: 42). As Hutton (2004: 235) concludes in her discussion of a later study of women's participation in the contemporary club scene, using ecstasy in club spaces served to help women feel 'empowered and positive about their own identities' and '[t]he experience of taking "E" was couched in terms of an exciting, enhancing, pleasurable experience and as part of a social event with friends'.

Hence, women researchers have challenged the view within drug use research of women drug users as passive, diseased, socially inadequate, polluted, unfit mothers, immature, morally weak and suffering from low self-esteem (Ettore 1992; Taylor 1993; Boyd and Faith 1999; Hinchliff 2000). Taylor's (1993) ethnographic study of the lives and experiences of women intravenous drug users in Glasgow is illustrative of this reframing of stereotypes. Her groundbreaking study presents an alternative, and refreshing, view of women drug users as 'rational, active people making decisions based on the contingencies of both their drug using careers and their roles and status in society' (p. 8). Similarly, Campbell (2000: 201) refers to the 'sense of autonomy and occupational mobility' and the resulting 'increased control over their own consumption' expressed by women participating in ethnographic studies on gender and drug markets in New York. These studies portray women drug users as 'economic actors' rather than emotionally disturbed victims.

Given the powerful ideology of reproduction underpinning women's role in society it is not surprising that women problem drug users who are pregnant, or those with children, have attracted so much attention both within the literature on women and drugs and in terms of policy responses. A review of the literature indicates that the issue of pregnancy, children and childcare is one of the biggest issues faced by women in dealing with their drug use (Henderson 1990; Sargent 1992; Taylor 1993; Boyd and Faith 1999; Heneghan 2000). Indeed, for Campbell (2000) the major difference in the experience of women and men problem drug users is their differential responsibilities for social reproduction – the daily business of keeping families together and afloat.

As primary carers therefore, drug use has significantly greater implications for women's relationship with their children than it does for men. Childcare concerns are inextricably linked with issues of stigmatization, and these become particularly acute for women during pregnancy. Stigmatization resulting from their violation of traditional roles and gender expectations, along with prejudice regarding their fitness as parents, threaten women's continued care of their children to a much greater extent than in the case of men. Research has shown that issues of child protection and fear of their children being placed in local authority care prevent women from approaching drugs services, and in particular statutory services (Henderson 1990; Sargent 1992; Taylor 1993; Klee 1998; Institute for the Study of Drug Dependence 1999; Heneghan 2000; Painter et al. 2000; Powis et al. 2000; Becker and Duffy 2002). On the other hand, Swift et al. (1996) found that concern over their children's welfare can be a motivating force for women to seek help with their problem drug use. Gossop (2003) refers to the uncomfortable dilemma faced by women in seeking treatment, knowing that this might serve to avoid *or* increase the risk of their children being taken into care. Clarke and Formby (2000) refer to research that suggests that this fear also acts as a deterrent for pregnant drug users in respect of antenatal services. According to Klee (2002: 4), the situation has not changed in recent years. This fear is fuelled by what she describes as 'the condemnatory and stigmatising judgements regarding pregnant drug users to be found in the media, the law and amongst the general public'.

Some studies of women's drug use have attempted to move beyond a concern with the negative implications for reproduction and children. Taylor's (1993) study, for example, focuses on the experiences of women who actively engage in drug-using careers and how this activity serves to increase their independence despite the cost of being viewed as inadequate mothers. Her study offers a consideration of children as both a motivating factor for change in their mothers' drug use and as variables in their mothers' continued drug use – a finding supported by research elsewhere (Swift *et al.* 1996; Elliott and Watson 2000). Klee (1998) reports on women drug users' perceptions of the positive aspects of drug use for parents with childcare responsibilities. In presenting research findings as part of an analysis of the stereotypes of drug-using parents, she discusses the value respondents placed on their use of amphetamines in helping them to cope with these responsibilities.

Working towards gender-sensitive policy responses

A gender-sensitive approach towards understanding drug users could be used to inform the development of enhanced services for both men and women (Broom 1995), and is particularly important for women whose lives are being directly influenced by gender issues such as pregnancy and motherhood (Wright 2002: 27). The theoretical discussion of women's illicit drug use offered above highlights three key considerations for developing gender-sensitive policy responses: a strategic approach, a structural analysis and an empowering approach.

A strategic approach

Klee (2002: 10) is critical of the lack of progress in translating what is now a widespread recognition for services to address women's needs in drugs policy and evidence-based practice. She refers to a 'lack of training and clear unambiguous policy', along with a 'lack of empirically based data on parenting by drug users' as the main hindrance to making progress in this area. In their recommendations, Becker and Duffy (2002) argue for a strategic approach to the development of services for women problem drug users. They identify the need for improved inter-agency working as a means of addressing the complex needs of this group. This recognizes the significance for women of the links between their drug use and their health, education, social (including recreational), financial, housing, legal and employment needs, and that problem drug use cannot be tackled in isolation from women's other needs. Interestingly, Becker and Duffy note that women problem drug users are highlighted as a special group, particularly in relation to their parenting role, in the NTA consultation on integrated care models. The implementation of integrated care pathways, which is a key aspect of these models, appears to offer the potential for more effective inter-agency working. The prevalence of mental health and sexual health problems among women problem drug users (Gossop 2003) and past traumatic experience of childhood abuse or domestic violence (Klee 2000) would, for instance, require joint or collaborative working between a range of professionals and services. Similarly, the high numbers of women problem drug users in prison calls for collaborative working between the criminal justice system and health and social care agencies, community drugs agencies and generic services in planning appropriate throughcare on release.

A structural analysis

While Becker and Duffy (2002) refer to the association between drug use and environmental and socioeconomic factors, such as unemployment and homelessness, their report does not explore the particular relationship women have with poverty and nor do they highlight this as a 'distinct issue' for women problem drug users.[2] In order to tackle the underlying causes of women's problem drug use there is a need for drug policy responses to embrace a structural analysis, and for such responses to be an integral part of policy initiatives aimed at addressing social exclusion. Noting the work of Hagan et al. (1994) in this area, Gossop (2003: 246) reminds us that '[m]any women drug users lack access to the economic and social resources required to remove themselves from abuse and chaotic or oppressive situations'. In discussing the association for women between drug use and prostitution, Boyd and Faith (1999) suggest that the real issue for women who engage in sex work is poverty and lack of perceivable options. Certainly research on crack-cocaine use suggests that it cannot be addressed in isolation from the poverty and lack of opportunity experienced by its users and their communities (Campbell 2000; Harwick and Kershaw 2003).

Within a feminist analysis, Ettore (1992) argues the need for an epistemology of substance misuse that is mindful of the experiences of women as

---

2   Other than in the context of women's mental health needs.

a social group. She cautions against ignoring sexual divisions and failing to make the link between substance misuse and the overall structural dynamics of power and dependency. Wright (2002: 17) calls for the need for further research on the effect of interpersonal relationships. She highlights research indicating women problem drug users' greater likelihood of having a drug-using partner and research that both supports and challenges the stereotype of 'passive women pressured into using drugs by their partners'. Similarly, the traditional view that women rely on men for the supply of drugs has been challenged. Taylor (1993) presents findings that indicate women are becoming more assertive and that they are as independent as men in maintaining their drug dependency. She reveals that women often finance their drug use themselves and in doing so run the same risks as male drug users. Taylor's research also differs in its findings on the link between women's drug use and commercial sex work. While a number of studies suggest that some women problem drug users use sex work as a means to support their dependency,[3] Taylor found that sex work was not widely used as a source of funding.

An empowering approach

While applauding the need to pay attention to gender and the need for gender-specific policy responses, the nature of this relationship also matters (Campbell 2000). Malloch (2000) warns of the implications of a discourse dominated by images of criminality and disease that portrays women problem drug users as more deviant and disturbed than men. There is a risk that policies reflecting popular cultural attitudes about women's problem drug use as deviant, irresponsible and potentially harmful to children may make women more vulnerable to adverse legal intervention instead of a policy of harm reduction. Campbell (2000: 17) argues for policy responses that 'explicitly attend to women's rights, well-being, and autonomy', and for an understanding of the relationship between women's drug use and issues of social exclusion, stigmatization and inequity.

Conclusion

The growing focus on gender provides important knowledge on drug use between women and men in twenty-first century Britain and also within different cultures of drug use. This is helpful in developing future policy responses. This chapter reinforces the need for what Henderson (1999) calls a new 'gender and drug use paradigm' – one that recognizes changing trends and patterns of women's and men's drug use in relation to the broader

---

3   Becker and Duffy (2002) identify research investigating the relationship between drug use and sex work.

changes in the social definition of gender and gender roles. Trends in drug policy indicate a shift towards a more flexible response with an inter-agency focus. This is particularly evident in the national service framework providing models of care. With or without this framework, however, it is clear that drugs policy can only effectively meet the diverse needs of women and men who use drugs if it embraces and challenges the many other areas of social policy that impinge upon their lives.

References

ACMD (Advisory Council on the Misuse of Drugs) (1989) *AIDS and Drug Misuse: Part Two*. London: Her Majesty's Stationery Office.

ACMD (Advisory Council on the Misuse of Drugs) (1998) *Drug Misuse and the Environment*. London: Stationery Office.

Barber, J. G. (1995) *Social Work with Addictions*. Basingstoke: Macmillan.

Beale, J. (2004) Gender and illicit drug use, *British Journal of Social Work*, 34: 851–70.

Becker, J. and Duffy, C. (2002) *Women Drug Users and Drugs Service Provision: Service-level Responses to Engagement and Retention*. London: Home Office Drugs Strategy Directorate.

Boyd, S, and Faith, K. (1999) Women, illegal drugs and prison: views from Canada, *International Journal of Drug Policy*, 10: 195–207.

Broom, D.H. (1995) Rethinking gender and drugs, *Drug and Alcohol Review*, 14: 411–15.

Campbell, N.D. (2000) *Using Women: Gender, Drug Policy and Social Justice*. London: Routledge.

Clarke, K. and Formby, J. (2000) Feeling good doing fine, *Druglink*, 15: 10–13.

Collison, M. (1996) In search of the high life: drugs, crime, masculinities and consumption, *British Journal of Criminology*, 36: 428–44.

Elliott, E. and Watson, A. (2000) Responsible carers, problem drug takers or both? in F. Harbin and M. Murphy (eds) *Substance Misuse and Childcare*. Lyme Regis: Russell House.

Ettore, E. (1992) *Women and Substance Use*. Basingstoke: Macmillan.

Ettore, E. (2004) Revisioning women and drug use: gender sensitivity, embodiment and reducing harm, *International Journal of Drug Policy*, 15: 327–35.

Ettorre, E. and Riska, E. (1995) *Gendered Moods: Psychotropics and Society*. London: Routledge.

European Monitoring Centre for Drugs and Drug Addiction (EMCDDA) (2000) *Annual Report on the State of the Drugs Problem in the European Union*. Lisbon: EMCDDA.

Gossop, M. (2003) *Drug Addiction and its Treatment*. Oxford: Oxford University Press.

Hagan, T., Finnegan, L. and Nelson-Zlupko, L. (1994) Impediments to comprehensive treatment models for substance-dependent women: treatment and research questions, *Journal of Psychoactive Drugs*, 26: 163–71.

Harwick, L. and Kershaw, S. (2003) The needs of crack-cocaine users: lessons to be learnt from a study into the needs of crack-cocaine users, *Drugs: Education, Prevention and Policy*, 10: 121–34.

Henderson, S. (ed.) (1990) *Women, HIV, Drugs: Practical Issues*. London: Institute for the Study of Drug Dependence (ISDD).

Henderson, S. (1999) Drugs and culture: a question of gender, in N. South (ed.) *Drugs: Cultures, Controls and Everyday Life*. London: Sage.

Heneghan, M. (2000) Race, women and treatment: alternatives to custody, *Druglink*, 15: 21–3.

Hinchliff, S. (2000) Mad for it: ecstatic women, *Druglink*, 15: 14–17.

HM Government (1998) *Tackling Drugs to Build a Better Britain: The Government's 10-Year Strategy for Tackling Drugs Misuse*. London: Stationery Office.

HM Prison Service (1998) *Tackling Drugs in Prison: the Prison Service Drug Strategy*. London: HM Prison Service.

Home Office (2000) *The Government's Strategy for Women Offenders*. London: Home Office Correctional Policy Unit.

Home Office (2001) *United Kingdom Anti-Drugs Co-ordinator's Annual Report 2000–01: A Report on Progress Since 2000 of the Government's Ten-year Anti-drugs Strategy*. London: Home Office.

Home Office (2002) *Updated Drug Strategy*. London: Home Office Drugs Strategy Unit.

Hutton, F.C. (2004) Up for it, made for it? Women, drug use and participation in club scenes, *Health, Risk & Society*, 6: 223–37.

Institute for the Study of Drug Dependence (ISDD) (1999) *Drug Situation in the UK – Trends and Update*. London: ISDD.

Klee, H. (1998) Drug-using parents: analysing the stereotypes, *International Journal of Drug Policy*, 9: 437–48.

Klee, H. (2002) Women, family and drugs, in H. Klee, M. Jackson and S. Lewis (eds) *Drug Misuse and Motherhood*. London: Routledge.

McGregor, S. (2000) *Drugs Research Funded by Central Government Departments: A Review*. Middlesex: Social Policy Research Centre, Middlesex University.

Malloch, M.S. (2000) *Women, Drugs and Custody. The Experiences of Women Drug Users in Prison*. Winchester: Waterside Press.

NTA (National Treatment Agency for Substance Misuse) (2002) *Models of Care for the Treatment of Adult Drug Misusers*. London: NTA.

Painter, J., Riley-Buckley, D. and Whittington, D. (2000) Practical considerations: making women's services available, *Druglink*, 15: 18–20.

Patel, K. (2000) Using qualitative research to examine the nature of drug use among minority ethnic communities in the UK, in European Monitoring Centre for Drugs and Drug Addiction (EMCDDA) (ed.) *Understanding and Responding to Drug Use: The Role of Qualitative Research*. Luxembourg: Office for Official Publications of the European Communities.

Perry, L (1991) *Women and Drug Use: An Unfeminine Dependency*. London: Institute for the Study of Drug Dependence.

Powis, B., Gossop, M., Bury, C., Payne, K. and Griffiths, P. (2000) Drug using mothers: social, psychological and substance use problems of women opiate users with children, *Drug and Alcohol Review*, 19: 171–80.

Raven, M. (2001) Developing skills in critical analysis of literature in the drug field, *Drugs: Education, Prevention and Policy*, 8: 191–202.

Sargent, M. (1992) *Women, Drugs and Policy in Sydney, London and Amsterdam.* Aldershot: Avebury.

Smyth, G. (2000) An exploratory study of issues which are relevant to recidivist women in prison with problem drug use. What are the implications for post-release support? Unpublished MSc Health Promotion Dissertation, University of the West of England.

Stevens, S.J., Estrada, A.L., Glider, P.J. and McGarth, R.A. (1998) Ethnic and cultural differences in drug-using women who are in and out of treatment, *Drugs and Society*, 13: 81–95.

Stimson, G.V. (2000) Blair declares war: the unhealthy state of British drug policy, *International Journal of Drug Policy*, 11: 259–64.

Straussner, S.L.A. and Attia, P.R. (2002) Women's addiction and treatment through a historical lens, in S.L.A. Straussner and S. Brown (eds) *The Handbook of Addiction Treatment for Women Theory and Practice*. San Francisco: Jossey-Bass.

Swift, W., Copeland, J. and Hall, W. (1996) Characteristics of women with alcohol and other drug problems: findings of an Australian national survey, *Addiction*, 91: 1141–50.

Task Force (1996) *Report of an Independent Review of Drug Treatment Services in England*. London: Department of Health.

Taylor, A. (1993) *Women Drug Users: An Ethnography of a Female Injecting Community*. Oxford: Oxford University Press.

Wright, S. (2002) Women's use of drugs: Gender specific factors, in H. Klee, M. Jackson and S. Lewis (eds) *Drug Misuse and Motherhood*. London: Routledge.

Further reading

Becker, J. and Duffy, C. (2002) *Women Drug Users and Drugs Service Provision: Service-level Responses to Engagement and Retention*. London: Home Office Drugs Strategy Directorate.

Campbell, N.D. (2000) *Using Women: Gender, Drug Policy and Social Justice*. London: Routledge.

Ettore, E. (1992) *Women and Substance Use*. Basingstoke: Macmillan.

Klee, H., Jackson, M. and Lewis, S. (eds) (2002) *Drug Misuse and Motherhood*. London: Routledge.

Malloch, M.S. (2000) *Women, Drugs and Custody. The Experiences of Women Drug Users in Prison*. Winchester: Waterside Press.

Taylor, A. (1993) *Women Drug Users: An Ethnography of a Female Injecting Community*. Oxford: Oxford University Press.

chapter

three

Young People and Drugs

Margaret Melrose

Introduction

At the time of writing, it seems that hardly a month passes without a new policy initiative in relation to young people and drugs. This chapter argues that the development of drug policy in relation to young people cannot be understood in isolation from developments in other policy areas, for example in welfare rights and juvenile justice. It suggests that contemporary concerns with young people and their drug use cannot be separated easily from broader concerns with youth crime or from broader policy developments in relation to young people's welfare rights. The chapter argues that policies that have been pursued over the past 25 years have progressively impoverished, criminalized and disenfranchised many young people and that policy initiatives that have been developed to respond to their drug use should be understood in this context.

Before discussing the development of drug policy in relation to young people, the chapter explores definitions of 'young people' and 'drugs' and raises questions about which young people, what drugs and what types of drug use are being referred to in policy debates about young people and drugs. It then explores the background to young people moving into the drug policy arena before examining the development of drug policy in relation to young people. It suggests that in this field, as in many others, the social policy agenda is driven by concerns with crime and community safety (Barton 1999) or what Pitts (2000: 10) has described as 'the politics of electoral anxiety' rather than by an interest in the welfare of young people per se.

Young people and drugs: the terminology

When is 'young' young?

The social construction of youth and young people takes place within particular historical, economic, political and ideological contingencies and material conditions. In the past 25 years, definitions of youth and young people have become increasingly slippery as they have been used to serve different institutional arrangements and ideological requirements. In terms of the Children Act 1989, for example, young people are defined as anyone up to the age of 18. If the young person has been in the looked-after system, they may be defined as a child in need who may be eligible to receive a service up to the age of 21. The Connexions service provides for young people aged 16–19 years. In the debate about young people and drug use, however, young people have been institutionally, if not legally, redefined. The government's ten-year drug strategy, for example, uses the term to describe anyone up to the age of 25 (President of the Council 1998). Even in academic texts that discuss young people and drug use, we find the term young people employed within the same paragraph to describe those aged 16–29 as well as those aged 15–16 (Parker *et al.* 2001: 2).

The reconstruction of 'the young' in the debate about drug use is paralleled by their reconstitution in the field of welfare entitlements. Here, a young person is defined as anyone up to the age of 25 (or 26 if they are claiming housing benefit). They are eligible for a reduced level of state support until they reach this age regardless of their needs, responsibilities or social situations (Coles and Craig 1999). Those aged 16 and 17 are no longer eligible for support unless in exceptional circumstances (Dean 1997). Where youth ends and adulthood begins has therefore become increasingly unclear as young people and their social rights have been institutionally and materially redefined over the years. Such redefinitions are used to serve different purposes and fulfil different ideological roles.

Clearly, all young people do not experience youth in the same way but this is less a function of their age than of the structural conditions of class, gender, ethnicity and sexuality within which the nature of particular childhoods is determined (Goldson 1997). As a result of the abstruse economic and social changes that have occurred in Britain in the past 25 years, the experiences of children and young people are increasingly polarized (Johnston *et al.* 2000; Goldson *et al.* 2002). So disparate are these experiences some suggest it is now more appropriate to talk about a variety of youths rather than of youth as a single and universal phenomenon (James and Prout 1990 cited in Goldson 1997).

These profound social and economic transformations have meant that some young people have literally been prevented from growing up. They are unable to make the transition to employment, homes and families on their own because they simply do not have the means to do so. They have become stuck in what has been described as 'a perpetual state of adolescence' (Pitts 2001). Often, these young people may be 'living on the margins' of society (Blackman 1997) and it is often those who inhabit these margins who tend to be found at the heavy end of the drug use/misuse spectrum (Melrose 2000; Parker *et al.* 2001; Melrose 2004). This chapter suggests that these young people have been 'othered' as a result of their position on the margins and thus it is they, rather than the generality of 'youth', who have become the objects of drug policy interventions in recent years.

Drugs

If the concept of young people is muddied, the concept of drugs is no less clear. The historical and cultural variability of moral and political judgements that determine what drugs are rendered illicit at any given time means the concept of drugs lacks scientific validity and is neither unproblematic nor value-free (Ruggerio 1999; South 1999). There is a vast array of illicit substances available for use and/or abuse in contemporary society and to lump these together under the term 'drugs' tends to obscure more than it reveals. To base policy on this aggregate concept lacks the subtlety that might be required for a drug policy to work successfully (Parker *et al.* 1998; Parker *et al.* 2001).

It is necessary to distinguish between different types of drugs and different kinds of use for the following reasons:

- varied cultures of use surround particular types of drugs and groups of young people use different drugs for distinct purposes;
- levels and frequency of use vary depending on what drugs we are talking about, including the context in which they are used and the purpose for which they are being used (Parker *et al.* 1998; Melrose 2000);
- different drugs have distinct effects on users and may be more or less harmful both for those who use them and their surrounding communities (Parker *et al.* 2001), and
- evidence suggests that young people view drug use more or less seriously depending on the type of drugs involved (Melrose 2000).

A considerable body of work suggests that young people may experiment with drugs during adolescence but that they tend to grow out of drugs as they proceed to adulthood (Advisory Council on the Misuse of Drugs (ACMD) 1998; Measham *et al.* 1998; Newburn 1999; Melrose 2000; Ward *et al.* 2003). Young people tend to modify their drug use over time and early teenage experimentation with illicit drugs need not, therefore, *necessarily* be a cause for major concern. However, this depends on the drugs used, how they were introduced, reason(s) for use and the broader context (Melrose 2000).

It is therefore helpful to distinguish between drug *use* – which allows the young person to continue with usual social life – and drug *misuse* which interferes with normal social functioning (Standing Conference on Drug Abuse (SCODA) 1997). Similar distinctions are made between recreational users and heavy end users (Parker *et al.* 1998, 2001). Using this distinction, we may acknowledge there may be many young recreational drug *users* but a much smaller number who *misuse* drugs. Research suggests that those who *use* and those who *misuse* drugs tend to be different in terms of social class and social location (Parker *et al.* 2001).

The New Labour ten-year anti-drug strategy distinguishes drugs such as cocaine and heroin from other drugs such as cannabis. The strategy acknowledges that the former cause the most harm both to the users and the communities in which they live (President of the Council 1998). Nevertheless, in general terms, the drug strategy appears not to distinguish recreational drug users from what have been described as heavy end users, notably people using crack, cocaine and/or heroin) (Parker *et al.* 1998, 2001) and neither does it distinguish drug use from misuse (Gould 2001). These distinctions are important especially when formulating policy.

The background to young people entering the drug policy debate

During the 1980s and into the 1990s, profound changes occurred in relation to drug use among young people and two parallel, if not overlapping, trends could be discerned. On the one hand, during the 1980s, recreational drug use (cannabis, ecstasy, amphetamine and lysergic acid diethylamide (LSD)) was increasing and changing (Parker *et al.* 2001: 3) in mainstream youth culture. So widespread had recreational drug use become that some commentators suggested it had become 'normalized' in mainstream youth culture (Parker *et al.* 1998; South 1999). By the government's own admission, there were more young people using drugs in the UK than in any other European country (National Strategy for Neighbourhood Renewal (NSNR) 2000).

The arguments that drug use had become 'normalized' in youth culture were first advanced by Parker *et al.* (1995, 1998). They (1998: 151) suggest the extraordinary increase in recreational drug use was 'deeply embedded' in other social processes which altered the experience of growing up in the late modern age. The normalization thesis refers to widespread recreational use of particular types of drug – especially cannabis but also amphetamines, LSD and ecstasy. South (1999: 5) suggests that '*awareness* and *ideas* about drugs have been changing' as drugs are now so widespread and 'it is non-acquaintance with drugs or drug users that has become the deviation from the norm'. Parker *et al.* (1998: 1) suggest that such widespread drug use can no longer be accounted for by employing 'pathologising explanations'.

The 'normalization' thesis, however, is challenged by others, including Shiner and Newburn (1999: 142) who suggest that assertions that drug use is widespread in youth culture are 'exaggerated and inaccurate'. Drawing on analysis of the British Crime Survey and the Youth Lifestyle Survey, Shiner and Newburn (1999) show that while 36 per cent of 16–19-year-olds and 33 per cent of 14–25-year-olds had ever used cannabis, only 29 per cent of the former and 22 per cent of the latter had used cannabis in the last year. These figures, they argue, do not support the claim that drug use among young people is 'normalized' (Shiner and Newburn 1999: 145). Additionally, Shiner and Newburn (1999: 152) present evidence to suggest that many young people still hold restrictive attitudes towards drugs and drug users and that 'drugs are generally ordered in some hierarchy of disapproval'.

Whether or not a process of normalization has occurred or is occurring in relation to drug use, it is clear that the availability of drugs has increased (Parker *et al.* 1995, 1998, 2001; President of the Council 1998; Shiner and Newburn 1999; South 1999; National Strategy for Neighbourhood Renewal 2000; Working Party of the Royal College of Psychiatrists and the Royal College of Physicians 2000; Burke 2004). Thus, while recreational drug use was moving onto the centre stage of mainstream youth culture, a parallel development was taking place in the culture of marginalized youth in relation to heroin (Dorn and South 1987; Parker *et al.* 2001). At this time an epidemic of heroin use developed (Pearson 1999) which some suggest has since become endemic in some parts of the UK (Parker *et al.* 2001). In the four-year period from 1981–5, for example, the Home Office was notified of 21,030 new addicts, many of whom were aged under 25 (British Youth Council 1992; South 1997).

These 'new' heroin users tended initially to be young (18–25 years), male and socially disadvantaged (Parker *et al.* 2001: 4). Heroin use had left the confines of the professional classes in London and the South East to become a working-class youth phenomenon across the country (Parker *et al.* 2001; Pitts 2001). A new outbreak of heroin use among socially disadvantaged people developed alongside long-term mass unemployment (Dorn and South 1987), particularly among young people (MacDonald 1997). However, drug use is frequently represented as a primary *cause*, rather than a by-product, of wider social problems such as unemployment and homelessness (Gould 2001). The question remains as to whether the increase in drug use by the young in the 1980s and 1990s in and of itself accounts for young people entering the drug policy arena, and remaining there since. This chapter suggests it does not and that, in order to understand this development in social policy, we need to explore other significant developments in relation to young people during this period.

Demonizing drugs and young people
Historically, drugs have provided plenty of raw materials for the creation of moral panics and young people have long been blamed for the ills of

society (Cohen 1973; Parssinen 1983; Kohn 2001). During the 1990s, the intertwining of young people, drugs and crime dominated domestic news (Parker *et al.* 1998: 5). The addition of danger to this chain of equivalence provided a 'potent mix' which evolved from 'real processes' (Parker *et al.* 1998: 7). These 'real processes' represented the increase in the number of young people using heroin and the arrival of human immunodeficiency virus (HIV) (Parker *et al.* 1998). By the end of the 1980s and well into the 1990s, a new danger hit the headlines warning of an impending 'crack epidemic' and of the 'threat' posed by young 'ravers' using the new designer drug, ecstasy. Such was the threat supposedly represented by these young people, they became the subject of legislation in their own right. The 1994 Criminal Justice and Public Order Act made unlicensed raves illegal and gave the police powers to stop the movement of people thought to be going to such events (Measham *et al.* 1998; Parker *et al.* 1998).

While moral entrepreneurs were busy establishing a chain of equivalence between young people, drugs, crime and danger they were simultaneously mobilizing other panics over young 'scroungers' and youthful 'barbarians' (Craine 1997: 131). Such panics enabled the Radical Right to identify economic hardship and social disadvantage as the creations of those who experienced them and served to confuse the social and economic consequences of what has been described as 'Sado-Monetarism' (Craine 1997: 131).

Acknowledging that problematic drug use tends to be concentrated among some of the most deprived groups of young people means that drug policies cannot be understood in isolation from other social policies. The epidemic of heroin use among the young that developed in the 1980s grew up alongside long-term mass unemployment. On coming to office in 1997, New Labour devised the New Deal programme to address the needs of unemployed young people. However, this has done little to create opportunities in the labour market (Tonge 1999). Rather, it has extended compulsion into a social security benefit system (Stepney *et al.* 1999; Theodore and Peck 1999; Tonge 1999; Jeffs and Spence 2000). As a consequence of the New Deal programme, young people's rights to receive welfare assistance from the state have been tied closely to their work obligations.

As well as ensuring young people's participation in a fragmented, flexible and 'hyper-casualized' labour market through coercive techniques (Stepney *et al.* 1999), the New Deal for Young People dovetails with the government's intention to 'fight crime and the causes of crime'. Unemployment was identified as a primary target in the government's fight against youth crime for they believe that when people are integrated into the labour force they are less likely to become involved in criminal activity (Holden 1999: 530). The Connexions services for people aged 16–19 shares similar aims and involves street-based youth workers identifying, supporting, tracking and sharing information about hard to reach young people who are distinguished as those not in education, employment or training (Crimmens *et al.* 2004).

Fighting crime, and specifically youth crime, are central tenets in New Labour's political project (Pitts 2000) and have been high on the government's agenda since it came to office in 1997. The ten-year drug strategy announces its intention to 'break the link between drugs and crime' (President of the Council 1998) and to 'protect communities from drug-related anti-social and criminal behaviour' (Cabinet Office 1999b). The Crime and Disorder Act (1998) was the flagship piece of legislation intended to allow the government to achieve these objectives.

This Act emphasizes moral choice and responsibility, which effectively replace the idea that youth crime results from poverty, social inequality or psychological disadvantage (Pitts 2005). As Muncie (1999: 147) has argued, 'many of its provisions are explicitly directed not only at young offenders but at young people in general'.

The government's preoccupation with issues of crime reduction and community safety can be witnessed in many measures that have been introduced to respond to young people who may or may not be involved in drug use and/or offending. In 2003, the government introduced pilot schemes that would extend the provisions of the Crime and Disorder Act to young drug users involved in offending. These young people can be referred to an arrest referral worker at the point of arrest and/or be placed on a Drug Treatment and Testing Order (DTTO). Such policy developments have, it has been argued, introduced perverse incentives to offend (in order to get fast-tracked into treatment) for those (young and old) who require drug treatment. The measures have also had the effect of displacing out of treatment those who might voluntarily seek help in relation to their drug use (Barton 1999).

The success or otherwise of such programmes for young people, as for many others, is measured in terms of the extent to which the young person reduces their offending rather than whether a young person reduces or stabilizes their drug use. The latter measures would previously have been the yardstick by which interventions with drug users would have been deemed successful or not (Barton 1999). Evidence does show that problematic drug users are responsible for a disproportionate amount of crime – usually acquisitive crime (Edmunds *et al.* 1998). However, they may not be responsible for as much crime as we may have been led to believe. Hammersley *et al.* (2003: 49), in their study of drug use among young offenders, for example, found that heroin use was 'more prevalent amongst medium frequency offenders than amongst high frequency'.

The introduction of DTTOs and Arrest Referral Schemes (ARSs) was intended to provide drug misusing offenders with 'the opportunity to tackle their drug misuse and reduce offending' (Cabinet Office 1999a). However, by focusing on acquisitive crime, usually engaged in by male drug misusers, these new policy initiatives tend to ignore young women who turn to prostitution to fund their drug use. Additionally, problematic drug users represent just a small fraction of *all* drug users and problematic users who engage in crime to finance their drug use represent a proportion of all problematic users.

Young people and drugs: the policy history

Berridge (1999: 279–80) has characterized drug policy in Britain in terms of four stages. The first, from the nineteenth century until the 1920s is described as 'open availability followed by pharmaceutical and medical regulation'. The second phase, from the 1920s to the 1960s is described as 'medico-legal regulation'. The third phase, beginning in the late 1960s, limited the right to prescribe heroin and cocaine to doctors who were licensed by the Home Office and who were attached to Drug Dependency Units (DDUs) which were also established in this period. In these early debates about drug control and the development of drug policies, young people did not feature. In the nineteenth century, when opium was widely and legally available, concerns were raised about the practice of infant doping but these tended to focus on working-class parenting capacities rather than on the actions of children or young people themselves (Berridge 1999).

The final phase in Berridge's chronology of drug policy development began in the 1980s. At this stage, a greater emphasis on penal sanctions was introduced into policy. However, during the 1980s the first recognition of the threat posed by HIV set alarm bells ringing and shifted policy in the direction of a harm reduction approach (Robson 1999). As Henderson (1999: 38) has argued, 'in the context of concerns about HIV and AIDS', drug use began to appear as a 'potential threat to the health of the nation'. It was at this time that young people entered the drug policy arena as objects of specific concern and they have remained there since. In this period young people were conveniently scapegoated by the radical right and, in the form of the 'underclass' or in the guise of young drug users, were represented as a threat to the established moral and social order.

Of the four stages identified by Berridge, it is possible to add a fifth, which dates from the 1990s. After initial scares about HIV had passed, policy moved away from harm reduction and back towards abstinence and zero tolerance approaches (Berridge 1999: 286). In this period, policy once again became more punitive, although harm reduction approaches were not completely jettisoned (Gould 2001: 226).

In 1994, after the failure of the earlier 'Just Say No' and 'Heroin Screws You Up' media campaigns to stem the increase of drug use by young people, the Conservative government launched its 'Tackling Drugs Together' initiative (HMSO 1994). This rested on three assumptions:

• young people are vulnerable to drug use as a result of peer pressure;
• drugs are both a danger and a threat;
• drug use poses a threat to local communities because drug users indulge in crime to fund their drug-taking.

These assumptions were, however, somewhat superficial and abstracted from a much more complex social reality. First, not all young people are pressured by their peers into taking drugs, but of course some are. Others actively seek out drug experiences (Parker *et al.* 1998; Melrose 2000). Second, some drugs (such as heroin, cocaine and crack) are more a danger and a threat than others (to both users and communities). Third, not all drug users indulge in predatory crime to support drug use but some do (Edmunds *et al.* 1998; Parker *et al.* 1998, 2001; Melrose 2000; Hammersley *et al.* 2003). These simplistic assumptions led to the generation of misinformation and, by suggesting that all drug use by young people would lead them into hopeless addiction and predatory crime, enabled the government of the day to link this drug policy initiative with their law and order agenda (Parker *et al.* 2001: 10).

The 'Tackling Drugs Together' White Paper recommended 'improved co-ordination and effectiveness at every level' (Gould 2001: 226). Recognizing the complexity of the drug problem, it called for 'a new partnership approach to dealing with drugs' (Parker *et al.* 2001: 10). Parker *et al.* (2001: 10) suggest that the creation of Drug Action Teams (DATs) was the most palpable outcome of this new partnership approach. These teams were designed to bring together representatives from key agencies, such as the police, probation, health services, education, social services and drug services to identify local problems and produce a corporate strategy, involving multi-agency initiatives, to respond to them.

When New Labour were elected to office in 1997, they continued the offensive against drugs when in 1998 they launched their ten-year anti-drug strategy (President of the Council 1998). The government also continued to link 'action on drugs' with its law and order agenda. New Labour's anti-drug strategy has four key aims, namely:

- to help young people resist drugs and fulfil their true potential in society;
- to protect communities from drug-related anti-social and criminal behaviour;
- to enable people with drug problems to overcome them and live healthy and crime-free lives;
- to stifle the availability of drugs on the street.

Parker *et al.* (2001: 11–12) suggest that this new strategy is both clear and appropriate, tending to emphasize prevention and treatment over 'crude enforcement measures'. By 2002, substance misuse education had become part of the National Curriculum and according to the government, 80 per cent of primary schools and 96 per cent of secondary schools had adopted drug education policies (UK Government 2002). In spite of this, a study published in 2003 found that in Birmingham 'between 30% and 40% of young people still felt they needed more information about drugs' (Fransham and Johnston 2003: 2–3).

By 2004 the government's drug education plans – a key component of its preventative strategy – looked to be in jeopardy. At this time, newspapers were reporting that the drug plan for schools had been abandoned as a result of a cash crisis. Such reports suggested that 'at least half of Britain's 150 school drug advisers . . . will be made redundant after central government funding for their posts ends in April' (*Observer*, 18 January 2004). Shortly afterwards, other reports suggested that 'the drugs message' was to be taught in every lesson. These reports related to guidelines produced by the Department for Education and Skills (DfES) which planned to integrate drug education across the school curriculum rather than confine it to health education lessons (*The Times*, 28 February 2004).

The ten-year anti-drug strategy also intends to 'reduce the proportion of people under 25 reporting illegal drug use in the last month and previous year' and to 'reduce the number of people under 25 using heroin' (President of the Council 1998: 15). In fact, to reduce the number of people under 25 reporting any illicit drug use and to reduce the proportion of young people using heroin and cocaine by 50 per cent by 2008 is a key performance indicator against which the success of this strategy is to be measured (Cabinet Office 1999b: 15–16).

The government's ten-year strategy promises to 'concentrate on those drugs that do the most harm' (heroin and crack cocaine) and would suggest that policy needs to concentrate on those young people who misuse such drugs. However, in order to achieve its goals, the strategy appears to rely on preventative measures since very little attention is given to the need to extend treatment services to tackle this type of drug use among young people (President of the Council 1998). In their study in Birmingham, Fransham and Johnston (2003: 6) found that: 'There was generally felt [among practitioners] to be a lack of provision at the Tier 4 level, for example a lack of detox facilities and residential rehabilitation for those aged under 18'. These findings do not appear to bear out claims made in the government's updated drug strategy (UK Government 2002: 7) that treatment services for young people 'including detoxification and community prescribing are now provided in 80% of Drug Action Team Areas'.

Conclusion

In formulating drug policy in relation to young people it is important to recognize that young people's drug use is highly fluid and likely to fluctuate over time (Advisory Council on the Misuse of Drugs 1998; Edmunds *et al.* 1998; Measham *et al.* 1998; Newburn 1999). Some may be more likely than others to initiate drug use when they are young and/or they may go on to develop more problematic levels and types of drug use than their peers

(Melrose 2000). It is also important to recognize the broader socioeconomic and cultural context in which this occurs.

Parker *et al.* (1998) suggest that for many young people, recreational drug use allows time out from normal role demands in work, education and their families. These young people are able to sustain assorted roles, consuming illicit substances in their free time then returning to their 'normal' roles. On the other hand, young people not in employment, training or education may find little to take time out from, having been excluded from key social institutions (Collison 1996). It is these young people who may be at risk of moving from drug use to drug misuse (Melrose 2000, 2004). That is, these young people may risk developing patterns of drug use that become entrenched and problematic for them, their families and their communities. In formulating policy responses to young people's drug use, it is therefore important to distinguish between recreational users and those whose drug use has become more entrenched and problematic. These represent two distinct groups of young people and a one-size fits all approach will not serve the interests of both groups. It is also necessary to pay attention to gender and ethnic differences in drug consumption patterns and trends.

The government appears to have made some progress in terms of preventative education for young people and this may in time reduce the numbers initiating drug use. However, in the field of young people and drugs, as in so many others relating to young people, it is the 'politics of electoral anxiety' (Pitts 2000) that appear to drive New Labour's policy initiatives. It seems likely, therefore, that policy in this area will continue to be driven by concerns about crime and community safety, as these are perceived to be the key battleground of electoral success (Pitts 2000).

References

Advisory Council on the Misuse of Drugs (ACMD) (1998) *Drug Misuse and the Environment*. London: Stationery Office.

Barton, A. (1999) Sentenced to treatment? Criminal justice orders and the health service, *Critical Social Policy*, 19: 463–84.

Berridge, V. (1999) *Opium and the People: Opiate Use and Drug Control Policy in Nineteenth and Early Twentieth Century England*. London: Free Association.

Blackman, S. J. (1997) 'Destructing a giro': a critical and ethnographic study of the youth 'underclass', in R. MacDonald (ed.) *Youth, the 'Underclass' and Social Exclusion*. London: Routledge.

British Youth Council (1992) *The Time of Your Life? The Truth about Being Young in 1990s Britain*. London: British Youth Council.

Burke, J. (2004) Drugs plan for schools abandoned, *Observer*, 18 January.

Cabinet Office (1999a) *The United Kingdom Anti-Drugs Co-ordinator: First Annual Report and National Plan*. London: Central Office of Information.

Cabinet Office (1999b) *Tackling Drugs – Government Action*. London: Cabinet Office.

Cohen, S. (1973) *Folk Devils and Moral Panics*. London: Paladin.

Coles, B. and Craig, G. (1999) Excluded youth and the growth of begging, in H. Dean (ed.) *Begging Questions: Street Level Economic Activity and Social Policy Failure*. Bristol: Policy Press.

Collison, M. (1996) In search of the high life: drugs, crime, masculinities and consumption, *British Journal of Criminology*, 36: 428–44.

Craine, S. (1997) The Black Magic Roundabout: cyclical transitions, social exclusion and alternative careers, in R. Macdonald (ed.) *Youth, 'the Underclass' and Social Exclusion*. London: Routledge.

Crimmens, D., Factor, F., Jeffs, T., Pitts, J., Pugh, C., Spence, J. and Turner, P. (2004) *Reaching Socially Excluded Young People: A National Study of Street-based Youth Work with Socially Excluded Young People*. York: Joseph Rowntree Foundation.

Dean, H. (1997) Underclassed or undermined? Young people and social citizenship', in R. Macdonald (ed.) *Youth, 'the Underclass' and Social Exclusion*. London: Routledge.

Dorn, N. and South, N. (eds) (1987) *A Land Fit for Heroin?* Basingstoke: Macmillan.

Edmunds, M., May, T., Hearnden, I. and Hough, M. (1998) *Arrest Referral: Emerging Lessons from Research*. London: Home Office.

Fransham, M. and Johnston, V. (2003) *Drugs, Young People and Service Provision: Findings on Needs and Services*. London: NACRO.

Goldson, B. (1997) Children in trouble – state responses to juvenile crime', in P. Scraton (ed.) *Childhood in Crisis?* London: UCL.

Goldson, B. (2002) Children, crime and the state, in B. Goldson, M. Lavalette and J. McKechnie (eds) *Children, Welfare and the State*. London: Sage.

Goldson, B., Lavalette, M. and McKechnie, J. (eds) (2002) *Children, Welfare and the State*. London: Sage.

Gould, A. (2001) Drugs and drug misuse, in M. May, R. Page and E. Brundson (eds) *Understanding Social Problems: Issues in Social Policy*. Oxford: Blackwell.

Hammersley, R., Marsland, L. and Reid, M. (2003) *Substance Use by Young Offenders: The Impact of the Normalisation of Drug Use in the Early Years of the Twenty First Century*. London: Home Office.

Henderson, S. (1999) Drugs and culture: the question of gender', in N. South (ed.) *Drugs: Cultures, Controls and Everyday Life*. London: Sage.

HMSO (1994) *Tackling Drugs Together*. London: HMSO.

Holden, C. (1999) Globalisation, social exclusion and Labour's new work ethic', *Critical Social Policy*, 19: 529–38.

Jeffs, T. and Spence, J. (2000) New deal for young people: good deal or poor deal? *Youth and Policy*, 66: 34–59.

Johnston, L., MacDonald, R., Mason, P., Ridley, L. and Webster, C. (2000) *Snakes and Ladders: Young People, Transitions and Social Exclusion*. Bristol: Policy Press.

Kohn, M. (2001) *Dope Girls: The Birth of the British Drug Underground*. London: Granta.

MacDonald, R. (1997) Dangerous youth and the dangerous class, in R. Macdonald (ed.) *Youth, 'the Underclass' and Social Exclusion*. London: Routledge.

Measham, F., Parker, H. and Aldridge, J. (1998) *Starting, Switching, Slowing and Stopping*. London: Home Office.

Melrose, M. (2000) *Fixing It? Young People, Drugs and Disadvantage*. Lyme Regis: Russell House.

Melrose, M. (2004) Fractured transitions: disadvantaged young people, drug taking and risk, *Probation Journal*, 51: 327–41.

Muncie, J. (1999) Institutionalised intolerance: youth justice and the 1998 Crime and Disorder Act, *Critical Social Policy*, 19: 147–75.

National Strategy for Neighbourhood Renewal (NSNR) (2000) *Report of the Policy Action Team 12: Young People*, London: Stationery Office.

Newburn, T. (1999) Drug prevention and youth justice: issues of philosophy, practice and policy, *British Journal of Criminology*, 39: 513–30.

Parker, H., Measham, F. and Aldridge, J. (1995) *Drugs Futures: Changing Patterns of Drug Use amongst English Youth*. London: Institute for the Study of Drug Dependence.

Parker, H., Aldridge, J. and Measham, F. (1998) *Illegal Leisure: The Normalisation of Adolescent Drug Use*. London: Routledge.

Parker, H., Aldridge, J. and Egginton, R. (2001) *UK Drugs Unlimited*. Basingstoke: Palgrave.

Parsinnen, T. (1983) *Secret Passions, Secret Remedies: Narcotic Drugs in British Society 1820–1930*. Manchester: University of Manchester Press.

Pearson, G. (1987) Social deprivation, unemployment and patterns of heroin use, in N. Dorn and N. South (eds) *A Land Fit for Heroin?* Basingstoke: Macmillan.

Pearson, G. (1999) Drugs at the end of the century, *British Journal of Criminology*, 39: 477–87.

Pitts, J. (2000) The new youth justice and the politics of electoral anxiety, in B. Goldson (ed.) *The New Youth Justice*. Lyme Regis: Russell House.

Pitts, J. (2001) *The New Politics of Youth Crime*. Basingstoke: Macmillan.

Pitts, J. (2005) The recent history of youth justice, in T. Bateman and J. Pitts (eds.) *The Russell House Companion to Youth Justice*. Lyme Regis: Russell House.

President of the Council (1998) *The Government's Ten Year Drug Strategy*. London: Stationery Office.

Robson, P. (1999) *Forbidden Drugs*, 2nd edn. Oxford: Oxford University Press.

Ruggiero, V. (1999) Drugs as a password and the law as a drug: discussing the legalisation of illicit substances, in N. South (ed.) *Drugs, Cultures, Controls and Everyday Life*. London: Sage.

Shiner, M. and Newburn, T. (1999) Taking tea with Noel: the place and meaning of drug use in everyday life, in N. South (ed.) *Drugs, Cultures, Controls and Everyday Life*. London: Sage.

South, N. (1997) Drugs: use, crime and control, in M. Maguire, R. Morgan and R. Reiner (eds) *The Oxford Handbook of Criminology*, 2nd edn. Oxford: Clarendon.

South, N. (1999) Debating drugs and everyday life: normalisation, prohibition and 'otherness', in N. South (ed.) *Drugs, Cultures, Controls and Everyday Life*. London: Sage.

Standing Conference on Drug Abuse (SCODA) (1997) *Drug-related Early Interventions: Developing Services for Young People and Families*. London: Standing Conference on Drug Abuse.

Stepney, P., Lynch, R. and Jordan, B. (1999) Poverty, exclusion and New Labour, *Critical Social Policy*, 19: 109–27.

Theodore, N. and Peck, J. (1999) Welfare-to-work: national problems, local solutions? *Critical Social Policy*, 19: 485–510.

Tonge, J. (1999) New packaging, old deal? New Labour and employment policy innovation, *Critical Social Policy*, 19: 217–32.

UK Government (2002) *Updated Drug Strategy*. www.homeoffice.gov.uk (accessed 28 March 2005).

Ward, J., Henderson, Z. and Pearson, G. (2003) *One Problem Among Many: Drug Use Among Care Leavers in Transition to Independent Living*. London: Home Office

Working Party of the Royal College of Psychiatrists and the Royal College of Physicians (2000) *Drugs: Dilemmas and Choices*. London: Gaskell/Royal College of Psychiatrists.

Further reading

Johnston, L., MacDonald, R., Mason, P., Ridley, L. and Webster, C. (2000) *Snakes and Ladders: Young People, Transitions and Social Exclusion*. Bristol: Policy Press.

Melrose, M. (2000) *Fixing It? Young People, Drugs and Disadvantage*. Lyme Regis: Russell House.

Parker, H., Aldridge, J. and Measham, F. (1998) *Illegal Leisure: The Normalisation of Adolescent Drug Use*. London: Routledge.

Parker, H., Aldridge, J. and Egginton, R. (2001) *UK Drugs Unlimited*. Basingstoke, Palgrave.

South, N. (ed.) (1999) *Drugs: Cultures, Controls and Everyday Life*. London: Sage.

chapter

four

One Step Forward, Two Steps Back? The Politics of 'Race'[1] and Drugs and How Policy-makers Interpret Things

Kazim Khan

Introduction

Important texts on racism and drugs from Berridge (1999) to Kohn (1992), Feuchtwang (1997), Murji (1999), Williams (1992), Bourgois (1995) and Reinarman and Levine (1997) remind us that public, media and official discourses on 'race' and drugs have been inextricably intertwined. Understanding this is key to any analysis of drug policy in relation to the UK's non-white, or, as they are referred to here, visible minority,[2] populations. Intertwining means that in these populations, drug users and non-users alike are vulnerable to a double stigma (Feuchtwang 1997) because, in some instances, discourses can construct them as hostile and inferior 'others'. As Kohn (1992) points out, displacement from one discourse to the other in popular (and populist) consciousness is as simple (and simplistic) as that from 'black' to 'crack'. It is my understanding that this historical intertwining continues to be specific to race-equality policy in the drugs field in ways that may obstruct progress. Thinking in this way also provides an appropriate starting point for an analysis of the policy challenges that lie ahead if UK drug policy is to effectively interlock with race equality. The first of these strands concerns the destigmatization of drug users, while the other stands for the destigmatization of visible minorities.

The other starting point for this chapter is the centrality of racism based on the classification of human populations into distinct groups defined by ethnic origin, race or culture or – in this example – skin colour, wherein each

1 Following an often used sociological convention, the term 'race' is used throughout the chapter as a social construct and not as a natural given. It is a convenient formula for deconstructing and discussing racism.
2 The term 'visible minorities' is used to designate people, because of skin colour and other physical features, in a racist manner.

such group is ascribed as possessing certain (selective) attributes. The path is then open either to discriminate against (or for) these groups on the basis of their presumed inherent characteristics, abilities and potential. Importantly, I suggest that surface 'celebrations' of difference ('diversity'), and its recognition in support of groups which define themselves on racial lines or by tokens such as 'ethnic' foods or black faces on posters ('multiculturalism'), do nothing to tackle the fundamental problem of racism and disadvantage. By enshrining and confirming the supposed distinctions on which racism is based, they risk perpetuating racism itself. To celebrate 'black culture' as vibrant and distinctive is still to accept an inherent difference based on skin colour.

This chapter approaches these issues through the recent history of policies and interventions (practices) intended to meet the care and treatment needs of visible minority drug users, and the education and prevention needs of non-drug users, from the same populations. Such a perspective enables changes to be linked to policies and an assessment of those which have proved effective and others which might be understood as ineffective. It is written from the point of view of a central actor in, and observer and researcher of, those developments and experiences and documents which have yet to be subject to systematic academic enquiry.

We begin with the first stirrings of an awareness of visible minority drug users and the resultant responses, and show that these have tended to be local and *ad hoc* rather than emerging from any stated policy by government or other bodies. The forces lobbying for recognition of the needs of visible minority drug users, in particular the Black Drug Workers' Forum (BDWF) are considered, and a brief mention is made of the beginnings of community-based action research. The chapter then moves on to analyse the beginnings of policy-making on race and drugs, casting a critical eye over the silences and the responses. It concludes with an analysis of the currently emerging UK drugs and diversity strategy and outlines what a just and equitable strategic response might look like.

This study is also divided into distinct periods, with the last quarter of the previous century forming a kind of pre-history to the period roughly from 2000 to the present day. The first period, 1975–99, coincides principally with the expansion of drug services, the beginnings of 'serious' government drug policy formulation, and the establishment of a UK Anti-Drugs Coordination Unit (UKADCU), followed by the creation of the office of the Drugs Czar. It closes with the abandonment of this office and reversion to a twin-track crime/health strategy. On the race-equality front, it overlaps with the enactment of the 1976 Race Relations Act (RRA), the first legal protection for Britain's black-, brown- and yellow-skinned populations.

The second period begins with the re-emergence of a twin-track drug strategy primarily anchored within the Home Office. It is coordinated by the Drugs Strategy Directorate (DSD), and within the Department of Health

(DH), where it is in turn coordinated by the National Treatment Agency (NTA). This is a specialist National Health Service (NHS) Trust, with the ostensible remit of setting standards for treatment. On the race front, this period begins with the Race Relations Amendment Act (RRAA) 2000 which lays statutory duties for public bodies to implement what may be briefly described as equality in the fields of employment and services.

Drug and race policy comes of age: 1975–99 – from invisibility to obfuscation: do blacks and Asians use drugs?

Today the question of whether blacks and Asians use drugs seems largely rhetorical – of course some of them/us do. Despite the fact that an observation was made as recently as 1996 (Task Force to Review Service for Drug Misusers 1996) upon the dearth of research in this area, there has since been a spate of action research, as well as in the Home Office scoping study (Sangster *et al.* 2002). But in the recent past the answers given by treatment services and by their funders, commissioners or planners sometimes, I argue, made it sound as if happy, healthy islands of non-whites could exist in a surrounding sea of white drug misuse to which they remained immune. Such responses were a measure of the low priority given to equality. A monocultural 'one kind of service suits all' approach, which in fact focused largely upon white male opiate users, was the stock in trade of the day. That there might be drug users and their families or friends who did not fit into this category, and who were not being accessed, did not register with policy-makers or with most specialist drug treatment and care services. This was both caused by and contributed to the hidden and unexplored nature of drug use among Britain's visible minority populations (Awiah *et al.* 1992; Abdulrahim *et al.* 1994; Task Force to Review Services for Drug Misusers 1996).

When visible minority drug use was recognized, the same dearth of data or experience allowed other myths to flourish: African Caribbeans favoured 'crack' cocaine; South Asians only used cannabis; both tended not to inject; their communities effectively took care of their own; and so on (Carroll and Johnson 1995; Sangster *et al.* 2002). No evidence was adduced for these racial stereotypes, but their influence in the drugs field was attested to at the bi-monthly meetings of the national BDWF. I believe that at times both white and visible minority drug workers fed into these myths (they still do), often as a means of tapping into scarce funds.

Race equality policies and practices in the wake of the 1976 RRA: multiculturalism vs. race equality

Discrete fields of activity at times might give the impression of being insulated from the policy and practice issues preoccupying other sectors of society. The drugs field provides a clear example for my assertion. Drug users and, by association, those who care for them, have for long been stigmatized. Sometimes they have reacted defensively to the rest of society while being passionate advocates for the clients they serve. This introversion may explain why, in contrast to education, social services and policing, there was little change in the drugs field with regard to race. Of course, there were exceptions. Based on their understanding of race equality legislation, a few voluntary agencies took some proactive if *ad hoc* measures to meet the requirements of visible minorities, but in the main the drugs field did little more than reflect what was happening elsewhere in society, or more often, lagged behind. So to track race equality developments we must turn briefly to what was happening elsewhere.

Using RRA 1976 as a yardstick, what we see are fragmented, piecemeal and *ad hoc* adjustments to employment and service delivery in the education, employment, housing, social services, health and criminal justice sectors. Some, such as health, employment of visible minority staff and care of visible minority patients, have continued to attract criticism from the Commission for Racial Equality (CRE 1984, 1988). This may be because of the lack of direct accountability with some organizations, such as the NHS, when compared with others such as personal social services. In other areas, including housing, education and employment, the initiatives, in my view, were usually confined to ensuring these organizations kept to the right side of the law.[3] Any more actively pursued policies were varieties of 'multiculturalism' which did nothing in themselves to tackle racism and discrimination.

The failure of the softer or multicultural approach to deliver on race equality is confirmed by the findings of census reports carried out by the Policy Studies Institute. Successive censuses have documented the continued racial discrimination and disadvantage experienced by Britain's visible minorities in key areas such as employment, housing, education and health (Brown 1984; Jones 1993). In my view, at a conceptual level, non-racial categories based on 'ethnicity' and 'culture' were ushered in by policy-makers, implying that racism was only a matter of ethnic or cultural otherness, and that once this was understood, the problem would go away. However, I suggest that the problem did not go away. At a conceptual level,

---

3 The term 'canteen culture' has also been used by Macpherson (1999). This term refers to police canteen culture where the use of racial stereotypes and racist language referring to visible minorities was rife.

as at policy and practice levels, the multicultural approach was always heading towards a cul-de-sac. It seemed that so-called 'ethnic minorities', with their assumed baggage of ethnically or racially based 'cultures', were to remain for eternity as distinct others, always tolerated but never really accepted as equal citizens in a demographically fast-changing Britain. What I am suggesting is no more than what census surveys indicate: that there is *no* sphere whatsoever in British society – not in education, employment, housing, health, social welfare or policing – where visible minorities have been accepted as equals and treated accordingly. They have continued to be tolerated, yes, but as post 9/11 policies and interventions demonstrate, the limits of this tolerance are easily breached. As a Portuguese colleague observed, 'What you have in Britain looks like a softer version of apartheid' (personal communication).

Race equality in the drugs field: benign neglect and occasional beacons

Working against this tide was a few academics, researchers and practitioners. As early as 1990, it had been pointed out that racism was not directly tackled by multiculturalism or by funding visible minority community groups. Of course, these should be funded if they can become effective and accountable advocacy and pressure groups for the communities they claim to represent and work to end discriminatory or culture-blind practices. But it is racism rather than culture-blind practices which prevents the adequate recognition of a plurality of cultures in the allocation of resources, in schooling, education, the media, health and social welfare. Doing something about it depends on tackling standard, taken for granted practices which are discriminatory in effect if not in intention. At an organizational level, racism is not a unitary thing or an intention, but an outcome of practices such as an agency's human resources policy, its service development programme or its communications strategy, which combine to adversely 'impact on a category of the population that has already been classified in a racialist manner' (Feuchtwang 1987: 2). These can be specified in any one institution as it relates to its environment. This approach can be illustrated in studies of the police, schooling, immigration control, social services and the implementation of equal opportunities in employment (Cambridge and Feuchtwang 1990, 1992). For instance, the Race and Culture Policy Research Unit (RCPRU) focused attention on police 'canteen culture', and the operational effect of stereotypes in stops and arrests long before the Stephen Lawrence inquiry forced it onto the agenda of the Home Office and the UK's police forces. So too in the treatment or prevention of drug problems, each specific institution or field has problems of racism which are specific to it and which can be dealt with without having to await a general attack on 'race'.

Just what these were for drug services and the drugs fields as a whole remained largely unexplored and practice developments were even more piecemeal, *ad hoc* and patchy than elsewhere. A concrete indication of this neglect was the fact that enquiries made of the Standing Conference on Drug Abuse (SCODA) and the Institute for the Study of Drug Dependence (ISDD) during the late 1980s threw up very little knowledge or information about drug use among the UK's visible minorities. However, the former was the umbrella body for all not-for-profit drug services in England and Wales, while the ISDD housed the largest drug misuse library in Europe. For these two institutions not to hold any information at that time signifies a considerable gap in knowledge. Ethnic monitoring statistics from the Department of Health's Regional Drug Misuse Databases (RDMD), one of the key prevalence indicators, were also generally silent on ethnicity, or seriously flawed in the regions where this was recorded (Daniel 1991; Khan 1999a). The only other information was anecdotal and largely from the handful of black professionals working in the field. Consisting mostly of frontline workers, often working in isolation as the sole black worker in an agency, they came together to share information and provide essential support, forming the BDWF. Their frustration and anger helped catalyze movement on race and drugs, highlighting issues since confirmed by local and national audits, evaluations of drug services and action research.

The problem with much of this research was that it was rarely structured or contextualized within a race equality or even a multicultural framework or perspective. The earliest research articles and reports appeared in the early 1990s, after which the rate of publication gathered pace (Daniel 1991, 1993; Mirza *et al.* 1991; Coomber 1991; Penfold 1991; Adebowale *et al.* 1992; Awiah *et al.* 1992; Butt 1992; Perera *et al.* 1993; Abdulrahim *et al.* 1994; Carroll and Johnson 1995). Not surprisingly, these initial forays varied in quality and focus. Most uncritically accepted 'ethnicity' as an unproblematic given rather than as a social construct or a racialized euphemism for Britain's non-white citizens (see e.g. Awiah *et al.* 1992; Perera *et al.* 1993; Abdulrahim *et al.* 1994). Carroll and Johnson (1995) introduced the concept of 'diversity', a more clearly argued analogue of multiculturalism but one subject to the same limitations. Introducing some depth and sophistication to the emergent discourse, Mirza *et al.* (1991) highlighted the gender dimension and the hidden nature of black women's substance abuse, while Adebowale *et al.* (1992) and Coomber (1991) challenged the unproblematic givens too easily accepted in other work. Daniel (1991, 1993) questioned the ethnic data collected by the RDMD.

Government drug policy documents from this period also remained largely blind to race equality or were limited to a token acknowledgement with no accompanying guidance, advice or direction. This remained largely true even with the establishment of a cross-government coordinating unit for drug misuse policy (the UKADCU) and the publication in 1995 of its first strategic report (Carroll and Johnston 1995). The only serious policy consideration to appear in a report commissioned by the government was the responsibility of an independent task force (Department of Health 1996). While not going into detail, this did base its recommendations squarely on the 1976 RRA. Among these were: consultation with black and minority ethnic community groups and, importantly, actions which could be taken by service commissioners under existing legislation. Other reports (Adams and Khan 1993, 1997) also pointed out that the law permitted several ways of ensuring that drug care and treatment services were providing equitable access to visible minority clients, including stipulating such provision as a condition of a grant, contract or commission. That this went largely unnoticed by policy-makers, service commissioners, planners and providers indicates a lack of understanding of race-relations legislation and a lack of commitment by influential drug policy-makers and interest groups.

An example of the first evidence-based account of race equality practice in drug services

Research by Adams and Khan (1997) articulated what drug services could do on the basis of existing anti-discriminatory legislation. Interviews and questionnaires at 22 residential and day services in London with professionals (directors, managers and front-line staff) and service users found that race equality initiatives developed in a piecemeal fashion and were fractured and lagging behind other sectors in health and social care. Equal opportunities policies rarely moved from paper policies into operational and service processes, including human resource strategies. This lack of progress was in contrast to the desire for change expressed by the majority of participants who reported a need for:

- improved race equality infrastructure;
- greater commitment to equal opportunities from all professionals;
- positive attitudes fostered towards race equality among service planners, purchasers and commissioners;
- better planning and more community and user involvement on issues surrounding race equality.

The research found that while drug treatment services had a long way to go, when addressing the needs of visible minorities there was a reservoir of goodwill from which to draw upon. As we head towards the end of this period, race equality policy and practice in the drugs field appeared, in my view, to lag behind the progress made in respect of multiculturalism in other welfare fields. There were reasons underlying this state of affairs which, I argue, maintain today. These reasons will be taken up in the concluding section.

2000 to today: the Stephen Lawrence Inquiry, RRAA 2000 and the advent of 'diversity'

The racist murder of a young black teenager, Stephen Lawrence, in April 1993, and the much publicised incompetence of the police and the Crown Prosecution Service (CPS) in investigating the crime and apprehending the suspects, highlighted the lack of protection people faced against racial abuse (Cambridge and Feuchtwang 1992). The determination of Stephen's parents to pursue justice, together with public support and pressure, in particular from the black community, led eventually to a public inquiry chaired by William Macpherson. The aim of the inquiry was 'to identify the lessons to be learned for the investigation and prosecution of racially motivated crimes' (Home Office 1999).

RRAA 2000 and the drugs field

It appears that Macpherson and the RRAA 2000 had suddenly opened windows of opportunity for tackling race and addressing social justice. In the drugs field, for example, major race-related initiatives include those taken by the DSD and NTA, both of which now provide a good deal more information on race equality policy and practice and related issues. The NTA work programme, for example, includes a comprehensive race equality scheme. The scheme includes consultation, workforce planning, local area needs assessment, standards and accreditation, commissioning a pilot scheme for organizational reviews of diversity, and a scoping of research groups to design research strategy guidance. This should help community-based organizations to carry out needs assessment in their own communities and to become effective advocates with drug action teams around the commissioning of services. However, without evaluation it is impossible to confirm the effectiveness of this important initiative. Ongoing work suggests that delivery at ground level may turn out to be a case of *plus ça change, plus c'est la même chose*.[4]

Conceptual issues: drugs and visible minorities

Progress towards social justice for visible minorities depends on taking a series of steps designed to undermine the conditions of existence that nourish racism and other sources of racial disadvantage. As elsewhere, progress in the drugs field is hampered by diversions and obfuscations, occluding the central issue of how to tackle racism. 'Multiculturalism' dates back a generation, and is now joined by 'diversity', 'community cohesion', 'community

---

4 The more things change, the more they remain the same.

engagement', and 'cultural competence'. Adding to the confusion, conceptual and policy meanings do not remain static. In the past, in sectors such as education and social services, proponents of multiculturalism and anti-racism at times vehemently contested terms and concepts. In the process, differences between their respective means and ends became clarified, creating tangible and distinct approaches. Today, 'new management' allows for little such debate. Instead, meanings are glided over as if different terms are interchangeable. Such debate can come to be dislocated from the workplace, occupying the rarefied pages of specialist journals or websites. At a practice level, racism and other challenges are increasingly conceived of in ways which allow for the reinvention of policy to suit current fashions and political interests. Nothing better illustrates this than the clouding of race equality by the emergence of 'diversity' and the tacking on of 'cultural competence'.

Drugs and 'diversity' – diversions and occlusions

'Diversity' is central to the strategic concerns of the DSD and NTA, reflecting recent trends in the vocabulary of government policy across the board, yet definition is hard to find. None is provided by the DSD or NTA. The DSD Action Plan exemplifies the resulting occlusion (Home Office 2004). Diversity covers everything, but nothing clearly and in depth or with focus. The fault lines which might divide marginalized populations from the rest are mentioned – such as gender, race, sexual orientation and disability. Why any of these categories is covered by 'diversity' is not explained. If the aim is to find an omnibus term for different kinds of marginalization, this is not stated. In its present form diversity, at best, incorporates a diluted attempt to address race equality at the expense of moving away from terms like 'fairness', 'equality' and 'justice', and towards terms such as 'ethnic diversity', 'political correctness' and 'cultural consciousness'. The aim would appear to be to de-politicize race.

'Cultural competence'

In its *Models of Care*, the NTA (year) identifies 'culturally competent services' as an essential ingredient of effective treatment. The same concept is emphasized by the DSD in most of its work on diversity. This phrase gained currency mainly through a study commissioned by the Home Office Drug Prevention Advisory Service (Sangster *et al.* 2002: 26) which suggested that 'cultural competence – as it relates to the delivery of drug services' requires a number of elements (see Box 4.1).

A mixture of 'apple pie and motherhood' recommendations not specific to issues of race or culture, unrelated to competent service delivery, and of simplistic equations of race, ethnicity and culture, 'cultural competence' is, I argue, devoid of theoretical integrity. The NTA report offers no clear explanation for using it in preference to other approaches such as race equality. The (no doubt unintended) effect is to defocus from institutional racism and the measures needed to counter it. Replacing 'black' with 'white' clarifies the flaws in its recommendations, in particular the key assumption of who represents whom. For example, the requirement for 'cultural owner-

---

Box 4.1 'Cultural competence'

In its *Models of Care*, the NTA identifies 'culturally competent services' as an essential ingredient of effective treatment. The same concept is emphasized by the DSD in most of its work on diversity. This phrase gained currency mainly through a study commissioned by the Home Office Drug Prevention Advisory Service (Sangster *et al.* 2002) which suggested that 'cultural competence – as it relates to the delivery of drug services' requires a number of elements:

Cultural ownership and leadership (2002: 26) is said by Sangster *et al.* to be based on Khan (1999) and Fraser and Khan (1999). However this misunderstands and misrepresents those works. Nowhere do they emphasize the ethnicity in which the report's construction of culture is supposedly rooted. To the contrary, both works are strongly critical of the concept of 'ethnicity' and its limitations.

Symbols of accessibility (2002: 26–7) refers to cultural symbols including posters, leaflets and culturally-specific newspapers and magazines, showing that despite the report's attempt to distance itself from the multiculturalism of the 1970s and 1980s, it regurgitates the same ideas.

Familiarity with and ability to meet the distinct needs of communities (2002: 27–9) refers to the need to tailor interventions to the distinct cultural and religious traditions prevailing among different visible minority populations such as the centrality of family and issues of shame. But here 'culture' is reduced to 'ethnicity', and no acknowledgement is made of the problematic relationship between ideology, culture and personality, as lucidly depicted in the film *Yasmin*.

Holistic, therapeutic and social interventions (2002: 29–31) contains some interesting insights about, for example, the lack of professional counselling traditions in many non-European societies, but as a whole simply refers to an approach advocated by many services for white clients rather than one specific to race or culture.

Diversification of services (2002: 31–2) is a general argument for services to cater for poly-drug users, conflated with an argument for recognizing ethnic differences in drug use, which then undercuts itself by acknowledging that visible minorities are also beginning to use opiates and to inject.

Black and minority ethnic workers (2002: 32–4) is an argument for more visible minority staff at all levels of an organization, but has little to do with cultural competence and everything to do with equality of opportunity in employment, required by the RRAA 2000 to be integral to recruitment strategies.

> *Community attachment/ownership and capacity-building* (2002: 35) argues for drug services to involve local community-based institutions (churches, mosques, temples, etc., as well as community-based voluntary organizations) in partnership functions.
>
> This mixture of 'apple pie and motherhood' recommendations not specific to issues of race or culture, of employment measures unrelated to competent service delivery and of simplistic equations of race, ethnicity and culture, is, I argue, devoid of theoretical integrity.

ship and leadership' could lead to a search for groups which make their whiteness a key defining feature. A critique of the study has, among other things, drawn attention to problems inherent in matching clients and staff. Young, third- or fourth-generation visible minority people forge their own cultural identity which often eludes hard and fast ethnic categories. The point is not the delivery of a *culturally* appropriate service but an *individually* appropriate service which takes account of the full humanity of the client, including culture and heritage. Contrary to the assumptions of the NTA, there is a greater range of differences within any so-called racial or ethnic groups than there is between them.

Conclusions

Among the obstacles which need to be overcome if race equality is to become a reality in the drugs field, the first concerns what I understand as a lack of responsibility and accountability at the top of service management and policy-making structures. The importance given by the NTA and DSD to the study critiqued in this chapter is a case in point. It reveals the dearth of knowledge and understanding of race equality at the topmost level in the drugs field.

Any race equality policy needs to begin by focusing on institutional racism and on its conditions of existence. Therefore:

- the classification of human populations by ethnic origin, race or culture opens the door to racism by enabling it to be assumed that by virtue of this membership each individual seen as belonging to that group must be an essential bearer of its characteristics;
- government policies, in particular on immigration, feed on and reinforce nationalist or imperial myths of origin, as well as undermining race equality measures;
- classification practices, many of which are unstated, fail to address equality issues in the recruitment, promotion and selection of target populations and these practices are at work in different ways in different institutions.

During changing times and circumstances, these conditions interact to create new racializations. In our own day, this can be seen in the post 9/11 demonization of Muslims and Islam. This malleability means the conditions which give rise to racism must be identified afresh for each institution, but can then be tackled by deconstructing and reconfiguring those institutions. Until then, the drugs field will continue to construct and reconstruct the 'other' – the visible minority drug user – while evidence and common sense demonstrate that when it comes down to it, at base there is not much difference between white and non-white drug users.

If race equality is to be effectively addressed, it makes logistic sense that the agencies and agents for change have to be found among all the national population, including the majority population. Race does not solely concern itself with the legitimate interests and concerns of visible minorities, but is an issue tethered within the general struggle for social justice. It needs to be addressed by society at large (Khan 1999b). When white managers and policy-makers simply ask selected visible minorities what they should do ('consultation'), it creates the impression that white people have nothing to say and, therefore, have no investment in change.

The lesson needs to be learnt and understood and become second nature to us that if we demonize substances, we also demonize those who use them. And, not just those who use them but also those who are associated, often wrongly, with being the main providers and purveyors of such substances – the 'others', the visible minorities. An effective and pragmatic drug policy of this kind would begin to unravel the intertwined discourse of race and drugs, aided by a clear equality-based and openly and democratically arrived at policy that does not solely emphasize difference but which promotes social justice.

References

Abdulrahim, D., White, D., Phillips, K., Boyd, G., Nicholson, J. and Elliot, J. (1994) *Ethnicity and Drug Use: Towards the Design of Community Interventions*. London: AIDS Research Unit, University of East London.

Adams, N. and Khan, K. (1993) *Meeting the Needs of Black Drug Users in the SELHA Region*. London: Race and Drugs Project, City University.

Adams, N. and Khan, K. (1997) *Race-Drugs-Europe: Specialist Drug Services and Managing Change to Meet the Needs of Black and Other Visible Minority Drug Users*, Volume One, Cahiers T3E, No. 3. London: Race & Drugs Project, City University.

Adebowale, V., Cohrane, R., Ranger, C. and Coomber, R. (1992) *Substance Misuse and Ethnic Minorities: An Agenda for Change*. Northampton: Can Press.

Awiah, J., Butt, S., Dorn, N., Patel, K. and Pearson, G. (1992) *Race, Gender and Drug Services*, ISDD Research Monographs, 6. London: ISDD.

Berridge, V. (1999) *Opium and the People: Opiate use and Drug Control Policy in the Nineteenth and early Twentieth Century in England.* London: Free Association Books.

Bourgois, P. (1995) *In Search of Respect: Selling Crack in El Barrio.* Cambridge: Cambridge University Press.

Brown, C. (1984) *Black & White in Britain.* London: PSI.

Butt, S. (1992) Asian males and heroin use in Bradford, in J. Awiah, S. Butt, N. Dorn, K. Patel and G. Pearson *Race, Gender and Drug Services*, ISDD Research Monographs, 6. London: ISDD.

Cambridge, A.X. and Feuchtwang, S. (1990) *Anti-Racist Strategies.* London: Avebury.

Cambridge, A.X. and Feuchtwang, S. (1992) *Where You Belong.* London: Avebury.

Carroll, M. and Johnson, M.R.D. (1995) *Dealing with Diversity: Good Practice in Drug Prevention.* London: Home Office.

Coomber, R. (1991) *Beyond 'the black drug worker'*, Druglink, 6(3): 17.

CRE (1984) *Inquiries and Special Investigations, St Chad's Hospital, Birmingham Health Authority.* London: CRE.

CRE (1988) *Inquiries and Formal Investigations, South Manchester District Health Authority.* London: CRE.

Daniel, T. (1991) *Ethnic Monitoring and Drug Users*, Executive Summary No. 16. Centre for Research on Drugs and Health Behaviour. London: Imperial College.

Daniel, T. (1993) *Ethnic minorities' use of drug services*, Druglink, 8(1): 16–17.

Department of Health (1996) *The Task Force to Review Services for Drug Misusers.* London: HMSO.

Department of Health (2001) *Developing an Integral Model of Care for Drug Treatment–The Department of Health Models of Care Project.* London: Department of Health.

Feuchtwang, S. (1987) The politics of equal opportunities in employment, revised and published in A.X. Cambridge and S. Feuchtwang (1990) *Anti-Racist Strategies.* London: Avebury.

Feuchtwang, S. (1997) *The Threat to Care: Working at the Margins of Fear and Uncertainty*, Cahiers T3E, No. 5. Beauvais, France.

Fraser, P.D. and Khan, K. (1999) *Anti-discriminatory monitoring*, in N. Adams and K. Khan (eds) *Action Points for Change: Enhancing Quality Standards by Adding the Dimension of Race-equality*, T3E [UK]. Middlesex: University of Middlesex.

Home Office (1999) *The Stephen Lawrence Inquiry*, CM. 4262-I, vol. 1. London: Home Office.

Home Office (2004) *Drugs Strategy Directorate, Action Plan 2004–2005.* London: Home Office.

Jones, T. (1993) *Britain's Ethnic Minorities.* London: PSI.

Khan, K. (1999a) *Race, drugs and prevalence, International Journal of Drug Policy*, 10: 83–8.

Khan, K. (1999b) *Plaster over the cracks*, Druglink, 14(5).

Kohn, M. (1992) *Dope Girls: The Birth of the British Drugs Underground.* London: Lawrence & Wishart.

Macpherson, W. (1999) *The Stephen Lawrence Inquiry*, Cm 4262-I. London: The Stationery Office.

Mirza, H.S., Pearson, G. and Phillips, S. (1991) *Drugs, People and Services: Final Report of the Drug Information Project to the Lewisham Safer Cities Project.* London: Goldsmith's College.

Murji, K. (1999) *White lines: culture, race and drugs*, in N. South (ed.) *Drugs: Cultures, Controls and Everyday Life.* London: Sage.

Penfold, M. (1991) *Bridging the Gap: A Report on the Prioritisation of Services to Black and Ethnic Minorities and Women.* London: Community Drug Project.

Perera, J., Power, R. and Gibson, N. (1993) *Assessing the Needs of Black Drug Users in North Westminster.* Hungerford: Hungerford Drug Project/ Centre for Research in Drugs and Health Behaviour.

Reinarman, C. and Levine, H.G. (1997) *Crack in America: Demon Drugs and Social Justice.* Berkeley, CA: University of California Press.

Sangster, D., Shiner, M., Sheikh, N. and Patel, K. (2002) *Delivering Drug Services to Black and Minority Ethnic Communities.* London: Home Office.

Task Force to Review Service for Drug Misusers (1996) *Report of an Independent Review of Drug Treatment in England.* London: Department of Health.

Williams, T. (1992) *Crack House: Notes from the End of the Line.* New York: Addison Wesley.

Further reading

Cambridge, A.X. and Feuchtwang, S. (1990) *Anti-Racist Strategies.* London: Avebury.

Cambridge, A.X. and Feuchtwang, S. (1992) *Where You Belong.* London: Avebury.

Griffiths, P. (1998) *Qat Use In London.* London: DPI Paper 26.

Jones, T. (1993) *Britain's Ethnic Minorities.* London: PSI.

Kohn, M. (1992) *Dope Girls: The Birth of the British Drugs Underground.* London: Lawrence & Wishart.

Murji, K. (1999) *White lines: culture, race and drugs*, in N. South (ed.) *Drugs: Cultures, Controls and Everyday Life.* London: Sage.

Reinarman, C. and Levine, H.G. (1997) *Crack in America: Demon Drugs and Social Justice.* Berkeley, CA: University of California Press.

Williams, T. (1992) *Crack House: Notes from the End of the Line.* New York: Addison Wesley.

chapter

five

Drugs, Law and the Regulation of Harm

Michael Shiner

Introduction

> Looking back on the century's progress in regulating drugs, one does
> not have to be a free-floating libertarian to feel some sense of unease
> with the ways in which what was once a largely innocuous consensual
> market has become transformed into what is now routinely described in
> terms of a war zone. Rarely, if ever, can the penal powers of the state
> and international law have been used with such zeal to promote health
> and to protect people against themselves. Indeed, the concern with
> drugs and drug-related problems might well come to be seen as one of
> the more remarkable aspects of twentieth-century history – beginning
> with largely unregulated markets, innocent if sometimes indulgent
> habits and 'victimless crimes'; ending with vast and costly global
> law enforcement efforts, sustained levels of violence and widespread
> allegations of corruption, and drugs markets which are massively
> regulated but nevertheless rampant.
>
> (Pearson 1999: 478)

The notion that drugs should be subject to legal control is a relatively
recent development. For much of the nineteenth century, drugs markets
throughout Europe and North America were based largely on the spirit of
free enterprise, with little external regulation (Parssinen 1983; Berridge and
Edwards 1987; Jay 2000). In Britain, the first steps towards legal control
were taken with the introduction of the 1868 Pharmacy Act, which gave
pharmacists a monopoly over the distribution of opium and morphine
derivatives. Even by the end of the nineteenth century it was still the case
that cannabis, cocaine, morphine and heroin, complete with hand-tooled
syringes and injecting kits, could be bought over the counter from chemists

in Britain and North America (Jay 2000). Just a hundred years later, with global prohibition and the 'war' on drugs firmly in place, such arrangements seem almost totally unimaginable. How did this come to pass? What is the logical basis for prohibition? How should it be assessed? And what are the alternatives?

The rise of prohibition

Attitudes to drugs changed dramatically during the second half of the nineteenth century and it was, ironically, the pursuit of free trade that created a groundswell of opinion in favour of greater regulation and control (Kohn 1992; Jay 2000). In what came to be seen as one of the most shameful episodes in its imperial history, the British authorities sought to prevent the Chinese from enforcing a ban on imported opium. Although officially presented as a defence of free trade, the Opium Wars (1839–42 and 1856–8) generated considerable hostility and opposition. Exaggerated reports that China had been reduced to misery by slavery to opium emphasized the evils of the drug more vehemently than ever before and also prompted fears of revenge and reprisal. Thereafter, British and North American concerns about opium were inextricably linked to anxieties about the Oriental conspiracy and the corrupting influence of Chinese 'opium dens'. Alongside these anxieties, the rise of a powerful public health lobby, the emergence of an increasingly assertive medical profession and the growth of a burgeoning temperance movement all helped to redefine opium use as a problem (Berridge and Edwards 1987; Jay 2000).

By the early twentieth century, two distinct sets of views had emerged about how drugs should be regulated. Moral conceptions of drug use as a vice to be controlled by the law were challenged by a medical view of it as an addiction or 'disease' which required treatment (Berridge 1979; Smart 1984; South 2002). These different perspectives are still apparent today. In a recent review of international drugs policy, MacGregor (1999) distinguished between 'care' and 'control', noting that the balance between these approaches is evident in the degree to which drug users are managed through health and social care systems on the one hand, and the criminal justice system on the other. She went on to suggest that this balance provides the basis for dividing 'regime types' into the 'relatively pragmatic' and the 'more moralistic or ideological'.

The USA provides the quintessential example of a moral/ideological regime. It has a long history of prohibition, dating back to the 1914 Harrison Act, which has culminated in the 'war on drugs'. With recent initiatives such as 'zero tolerance' and 'three-strikes-and-you're-out', the US imprisonment rate for drug offences is higher than that of most western European nations for all crime put together (MacCoun and Reuter 2001).

European drugs regimes have typically been much more pragmatic and British policy has a long tradition of combining care and control, although the balance between these alternatives has shifted over time (South 2002; Spear and Mott 2002). Early controls such as the 1916 Defence of the Realm Act, followed by the 1920 and 1923 Dangerous Drugs Acts, criminalized the unauthorized possession of opiates and cocaine but permitted their possession under prescription from a doctor. These arrangements were formalized by the Rolleston Committee and provided the basis for the 'British System' which prevailed from the early 1920s to the late 1960s. There then followed a period of realignment as concerns about new and increasing forms of drug use led to a much greater emphasis on the role of the police and the criminal justice system (South 2002; Spear and Mott 2002). This initial shift was completed by the early 1970s and then reinforced during the first half of the 1980s in response to a wave of heroin 'epidemics'. By the mid-1980s British policy had come to be defined in terms of a 'war on drugs': central government had taken on a much more active role; the debate about drugs had been politicized; a new emphasis had come to be placed on law enforcement; and medicine had been displaced from its former central role (Stimson 1987). These developments were not challenged by any of the major political parties and a parliamentary consensus emerged which has been largely maintained ever since (South 2002).

The logic of prohibition

Drugs control raises important normative and empirical questions. What should be done? And what can be done? These are linked but nonetheless distinct questions, relating to the moral and practical logic of prohibition respectively. Moral logic concerns the philosophical justification for prohibition, while practical logic focuses attention on the operation of the law and on how it is that the law may be expected to bring about the desired outcome.

The philosophical basis of British drugs law is provided by the principle of harmfulness, which Ruggiero (1999) has argued is a paternalistic notion linked to a judgement about the wrongness of drug use. The state, or so the argument goes, has a responsibility to protect its members from causing harm, mainly to others but also to themselves. This principle was enshrined in the 1971 Misuse of Drugs Act which continues to provide the main basis of British drugs law (Police Foundation 2000). In an effort to ensure that the severity of punishment reflected the potential for harm, three classes were established (A, B and C) and drugs were allocated to them on the basis of the following criteria: whether they were being misused; whether they were likely to be misused; and whether the misuse in either case was having or could have harmful effects sufficient to constitute a problem.

Table 5.1 Legal classification of drugs and associated penalties under British law (1971–2002)

	Class A	Class B	Class C
Main drugs in each class	Cannabinol and cannabinol derivatives, cocaine (including 'crack'), dipipanone, ecstasy and related compounds, heroin, LSD, magic mushrooms, morphine, opium, pethidine and phenylcyclidine	Amphetamine, barbiturates, cannabis, codeine, dihydrocodeine and methylamphetamine Class B drugs that are prepared for injection are classed as Class A	Anabolic steroids, benzodiazepines, buprenorphibe, dietylproprion, mazindol, pemoline and phentermine
Maximum penalties *Possession*	7 years imprisonment or an unlimited fine or both	5 years imprisonment or an unlimited fine or both	2 years imprisonment or an unlimited fine or both
Possession with intent to supply	Life imprisonment or an unlimited fine or both	14 years imprisonment or an unlimited fine or both	5 years imprisonment or an unlimited fine or both

Source: Police Foundation (2000).
Note: The information given here includes additions to the classes that have been made since the introduction of the Misuse of Drugs Act: ecstasy, for example, was added in 1984 (Police Foundation 2000). Note that cannabis was transferred into Class C as of January 2004.

While distinguishing between the offences of unlawful possession and unlawful possession with the intent to supply, the Misuse of Drugs Act imposed progressively harsher penalties on each class (see Table 5.1).

The practical logic of prohibition rests on general theories about the role of law and may vary according to which approach is taken (Braithwaite and Pettit 1990; Ashworth 2002). According to a retributive approach, for example, punishment is justified on the grounds that it is the morally appropriate response to crime: those who commit offences deserve punishment and the amount of punishment should be proportionate to the degree of wrongdoing. Retributivism has been of marginal importance to criminal justice policy-making for much of the last century, however, and the role of the law has been more commonly conceived within the framework of a utilitarian-based preventionist approach. Such an approach has a number of different elements. It aims to incapacitate criminals in order to prevent them from continuing to offend (by locking them up, for example); it provides opportunities for rehabilitation; and it aims to deter those convicted (specific deterrence) and other potential offenders (general deterrence).

With its insistence on the greatest happiness for the greatest number of people, utilitarianism demands that the costs as well as the benefits of any intervention are taken into account. Given the financial costs of enforcement and the limitations imposed on individual autonomy, it can be inferred that no criminal law should be passed which does not *prima facie* have a good chance of achieving its (legitimate) purpose or is not necessary in order to achieve such an outcome (Lacey 1988). Inefficiencies arise where difficulties are experienced in enforcement or detection; where the law is ineffective as a deterrent; if the social and economic costs of enforcement outweigh the benefits; or if a less costly and more efficient means of enforcement is available. Inefficient and unnecessary punishment is an 'illegitimate' use of the criminal process and 'legislation which violates the principle of efficiency should be repealed or modified so as to comply with it' (Lacey 1988: 118–19). In addition, the principle of parsimony dictates that the state should be minimally interventionist unless there is clear evidence that more intrusive practices are required: 'Thus it is clear that the onus of proof ought to fall squarely on the side of justifying any such initiative, not on the side of justifying its absence or removal. The presumption ought to be in favour of less rather than more criminal justice activity' (Braithwaite and Pettit 1990: 87).

The revisionist critique

It is, of course, possible to accept the principle of harmfulness but maintain that current levels of punishment are disproportionate and that certain substances have been wrongly classified. This was precisely the position adopted by the Independent Inquiry into the Misuse of Drugs Act 1971. Established in 1997 by the Police Foundation, with the assistance of the Prince's Trust, the Inquiry aimed 'to assess whether the law as it currently stands needs to be revised in order to make it both more effective and more responsive' (Police Foundation 2000: 1). This assessment was based on the established harms perspective as the Inquiry endorsed the existing three-tiered legal framework and accepted that harmfulness should continue to provide the main criterion for classification. While maintaining that the primary justification for control lies in the harm that drug use causes to others, it argued that the law should also take account of the harm to users themselves. The potential for reform lay in the Inquiry's insistence that the present classification 'should be reviewed to take account of modern developments in medical, scientific and sociological knowledge' (Police Foundation 2000: 42).

Measuring the harmfulness of drugs is a complex matter (Best *et al.* 2001) and seemingly no explicit criteria were used for this purpose during the development of the Misuse of Drugs Act (Police Foundation 2000). While recognizing some of the associated difficulties, the Inquiry maintained that it is possible to reach an 'objective' estimate of the relative harmfulness of the various drugs. In the absence of established criteria, it distinguished between personal harm (made up of dangers for individual users) and social harm (made up of dangers for society in general), which were assessed on the basis of the following criteria:

- acute (i.e. immediate) physical harm, including risk of overdose;
- physical harm from chronic (i.e. longer term) use;
- ease with which the drug may be injected;
- likelihood of the drug leading to dependence and addiction;
- physical withdrawal symptoms;
- psychological withdrawal symptoms;
- risk of social harm through intoxication (including road traffic accidents);
- risk of causing other social problems (including crime);
- risk of medical costs arising.

The Inquiry ranked the main controlled drugs on these criteria using available evidence and, having consulted the Royal College of Psychiatrists' Faculty of Substance Misuse, divided them into three classes. Alcohol and tobacco were included in this exercise for illustrative purposes (see Table 5.2).

Two key points stand out from the Inquiry's classification. First, most controlled drugs are no more harmful than alcohol or tobacco and cannabis is less harmful than both of these substances. Second, the Misuse of Drugs Act overstates the relative harmfulness of particular drugs. In order to ensure that 'the classes provide a more accurate hierarchy of harm and

Table 5.2 Harmfulness of the main controlled drugs – Independent Inquiry

Class A	*Class B*	*Class C*
Cocaine, heroin, methadone, other opiates in pure form, amphetamines in injectable form and alcohol	Amphetamine other than injectable, barbiturates, buprenorphine, codeine, ecstasy and ecstasy-type drugs, LSD and tobacco	Cannabinol and cannabinol derivatives, benzodiazepines and cannabis

Source: Police Foundation (2000).
Note: For a detailed discussion of the harmfulness of the substances shown in this table please see Best *et al.* (2001).

commensurate sanctions' the Inquiry recommended that cannabis be ferred from Class B to C and that both ecstasy and LSD be transferred Class A to B (Police Foundation 2000: 4). Further calls were made fo. removal of the power of arrest for most cannabis possession offences and the abolition of prison sentences for most such offences.[1] These proposals reflected concerns about the inefficiency of existing law. The Inquiry concluded that 'demand will only be significantly reduced by education and treatment, not by the deterrent effect of the law' (Police Foundation 2000: 8) and emphasized that the need for reform was particularly pressing in relation to cannabis because existing arrangements produced more harm than they prevented: the identified costs included the financial costs of enforcement, damage to police-community relations and the criminalization of large numbers of otherwise law abiding, mainly young people, to the detriment of their futures.

The Inquiry made a somewhat awkward distinction between supply and demand, pursuing quite different forms of logic in relation to each. Although seeing 'no evidence that severe custodial penalties are deterring traffickers, or that enforcement, however vigorous, is having a significant effect on supply', it maintained that the law must remain the principal means through which supply is curtailed (Police Foundation 2000: 3). In practice this meant calling for a strengthening of the administration of existing laws against trafficking and the creation of the new offence of dealing. As such the Inquiry's recommendations are best understood in terms of a 'double taxonomy', whereby a shift towards liberalization is combined with an emphasis on increased control (Newburn 1992).[2]

The radical assault

Prohibition has also been subject to a radical assault, which can be traced back to the 1960s and the rise of 'new deviancy' theories.[3] Advocates of

---

1   The Inquiry rejected custodial penalties for possession of Class B and C drugs and proposed a shortened maximum prison sentence for possession of Class A drugs where community and treatment sentences had failed or were rejected.
2   Although the government's initial reaction to the Inquiry's report was very negative, cannabis has been transferred into Class C following reviews by the Select Committee on Home Affairs (2002) and the Advisory Council on the Misuse of Drugs (2002). This change came into force at the beginning of 2004 and reflected the double taxonomy described above (Trace *et al.* 2004): there is a presumption against arrest for possession and the maximum penalty has been reduced from 5 to 2 years imprisonment; but the maximum penalty for supplying Class C drugs has been increased from 5 to 14 years imprisonment, which has meant, in effect, that the penalty for supplying cannabis remains unchanged. None of the Inquiry's other major recommendations have been introduced.
3   For a contemporary version of the radical assault see www.tdpf.org.uk, the website of Transform, the Drug Policy Foundation, and www.dpf.org, the website of the Drug Policy Alliance.

these theories frequently expressed unease about the extension of social control into morally ambiguous areas and drew heavily upon the harm principle formulated by John Stuart Mill (1910: 72–3):[4]

> The only purpose for which power can be rightfully exercised over any member of a civilized community against his will, is to prevent harm to others. His own good, either physical or moral, is not a sufficient warrant. He cannot rightfully be compelled to do or forbear because it would be better for him to do so, because it will make him happier, because, in the opinion of others, to do so would be wise or even right.

This principle was reflected in the distinction that new deviancy theorists drew between crimes with and without victims. Duster (1970) and Schur (1965) developed the argument that drug use is a 'victimless crime' and, in doing so, challenged both the moral and practical logic of prohibition. According to Duster (p. 244) the use of the law to prohibit victimless crimes is bound to meet with very limited success:

> Drug use is engaged in privately, not publicly, and there is no party to the act who has an interest in being the plaintiff. For these reasons the law will not be effective in bringing about a change in behaviour or morality of the law violators. Thus, millions of dollars are spent in a fruitless attempt to stamp out the problem, that could better be used upon some constructive programme. At the very least, the negative gain would involve the elimination of the pursuit of an impossible task.

Schur (1963, 1969) went further, arguing that the use of the law in such a context is likely to be counter-productive. He was particularly concerned with the way in which North American drugs policy had created illicit heroin markets, arguing that prohibition had secured a kind of monopoly for suppliers who were prepared to break the law. By generating high prices, he argued, illicit markets had almost completely driven heroin users out of 'respectable' society and had pushed them into a subculture of crime and addiction: 'By defining him as a criminal, we have pushed the addict in the direction of becoming one' (1969: 213). A similar analysis was offered by Wilkins (1965) as he applied the notion of deviancy amplification to explain differences in heroin use in Britain and the USA.

The implications of the radical assault were developed most fully by Young (1971) in what was, in effect, an early formulation of harm reduction.[5] Young accepted that, in the final analysis, the most 'fundamental

---

4 It is a peculiar feature of the drugs debate that both prohibitionists and anti-prohibitionists base their arguments on this utilitarian principle (Ruggiero 1999).
5 Harm reduction describes an approach to working with drug users that focuses on minimizing the potential for harm rather than on eradicating use. Such an approach has been endorsed by the Advisory Council on the Misuse of Drugs (1984) and provides the basis for some 'treatment' interventions such as the provision of clean injecting equipment.

criterion of drug abuse is health risk', but argued that this did not mean people should be forced to avoid actions which endanger their lives: 'I am', he noted, 'in complete agreement with J.S Mill's dictum here' (1971: 222). From this starting point, Young went on to call for the restriction of legislation on the grounds that drugs law had proved damaging and unworkable. To legislate against victimless acts carried out privately and willingly, he argued, is fruitless and counter-productive as it creates a black market, increases drug prices and adulteration and invites criminal involvement. While recognizing that laws may be useful in protecting the consumer, Young emphasized that they cannot direct or stamp out consumer demand or illicit supply. In order to avoid a vast amount of unnecessary misery and hardship, he concluded, policy should concentrate on adjusting drug users' habits by suggesting alternative drugs or safer methods of use: 'We must learn to live with psychotropic drug use; it is only by treating citizens as responsible human beings that any sane and long-lasting control can be achieved' (1971: 222). Among the ten rules that he offered for a 'sane and just policy', the following are most relevant to the current discussion:

- *Maintain cultures:* subcultures which involve drug use often have a body of stipulations and controls which govern such behaviour and it is vital that drug use is enmeshed in a system of norms and controls if negative effects are to be avoided. To control the amount, type and administration of drugs requires sound knowledge accumulated over time and it is strongly dysfunctional to harass and undermine existing drug subcultures. In the cure of addiction or the treatment of bad trips, non-professional people from the respective subcultures are often more successful than medical professionals whose values are alien and knowledge sadly inapplicable.
- *Positive propaganda:* most information fed to the public about the nature and effects of drugs is misleading and inaccurate and this results in widespread scepticism. As young people learn from the experience of friends that the dangers of drug use are routinely exaggerated, the credibility of much of the literature and of traditional authority figures is lost. Members of drug subcultures become cynical about outside information. Given that law enforcement has failed to curb drug use, authoritative facts about the effects of drugs should be fed into the drug subculture itself, for it is the subculture of drug-taking which has the only viable authority to control the activity of its members. Information aimed at controlling drug use must be phrased in terms of the values of the subculture, not in terms of the values of the outside world.

Assessing critical claims

The moral case for prohibition is more complex than often implied and the notion that self-harm is insufficient to justify coercion can be challenged on a number of grounds. There are, as noted by the Inquiry, some situations where the use of the law to protect individuals from harming themselves is widely accepted. Legislation governing the use of seatbelts and motorcycle helmets provides obvious examples and such use of the law tends to be regarded as legitimate where the damage is serious, typically unintentional and hard to reverse. Illegal drugs are, to varying degrees, associated with precisely this type of risk and the case for intervention is arguably made stronger by the extent to which they reduce the power of choice (Police Foundation 2000). Laws against the non-medical use of drugs may also be justified on the basis that the criminal law seeks to protect fundamental interests in a dynamic way. Fundamental interests include such things as the ability to seek one's own welfare and exercise autonomy. According to Lacey (1988: 110): 'This gives a limited place for paternalistic legislation prohibiting the harm of inflicting or possibly even seriously risking grave, long-term and certain damage to one's own capacities for pursuing one's own future good'.

Finally, the very notion that drug use is a 'victimless crime' is open to doubt. According to the Inquiry, for example: 'it is impossible in fact to separate harms to users from harms to others; self-inflicted damage usually results in costs to others' (Police Foundation 2000: 43). Although the moral case is more complex than often implied this does not necessarily mean that prohibition is morally justified. Drug use may prevent people from pursuing their fundamental interests and may cause genuine harm to others, but this is only part of the equation. To be morally justified an intervention must prevent more harm than it produces and may fail to fulfil this criterion because it is ineffective and/or because it produces harm. In order to assess this possibility in relation to prohibition we must turn to its practical logic.

The practical case against prohibition is strong.[6] Drug use may not be a 'victimless crime' but, unlike most crime, it is committed with the consent of the 'victim', which makes law enforcement particularly difficult. According to Downes and Morgan (2002: 314): 'drugtakers actively collude in the criminalized process of drugs supply. By contrast, householders hardly invite burglars into their homes, any more than car-owners supply car thieves with the key, or victims of fraud knowingly supply fraudsters with their credit card details'.

The extent of the global failure of prohibition can be gauged from estimates which indicate that illegal drugs account for approximately 8 per cent of world trade, which is more than that in iron and steel and about the same as that in textiles (Elvins 2003). In Britain alone, an estimated £6.6 billion is spent on illegal drugs annually, which is only slightly less than the amount

---

6 Due to a lack of space the discussion presented here has paid little attention to the claim that prohibition causes *harm*. This claim forms an important part of the case made against prohibition, however, and details can be found at: www.tdpf.org.uk and www.dpf.org.

spent on cigarettes (Travis 2001) and the cost of drug-related crime is estimated to be greater than the Home Office's entire annual budget (Kushlick 2004). Even when the police are able to identify and arrest major drug trafficking operations there is no discernable impact on the price and availability of drugs (Drugscope 2004; see also Lee and South 2003).

According to Dorn and Lee (1999), such failings have created a sense of crisis in criminal justice agencies and have confronted nation states with the limits of their ability to regulate and control crime. In response to this crisis, they suggest, the police have adopted a 'containment' focus, within which an emphasis on the 'manageability' of crime and drugs has replaced 'the more heroic but politically risky "war" stance' (1999: 97). In Britain, for example, there has been a striking increase in the use of cautions for drugs possession offences and a sustained reduction in the use of fines (Police Foundation 2000). And the police have played an important role in the campaign for reform. The recent 'Lambeth experiment', where the police issued on-the-spot warnings for offences involving possession of small quantities of cannabis was given formal 'pilot' status by Scotland Yard and was described as 'sensible and progressive' by Sir John Stevens, then commissioner of the Metropolitan Police (*Guardian*, 15 June 2001). In addition, the Association of Chief Police Officers has endorsed the view that illicit drug use is primarily a health issue and that users should be treated rather than punished (*Daily Mail*, 2 May 2002).

Under these circumstances to maintain, as the United Nations (1998) has, that 'a drug free world' is viable option must strain the credulity of all but the most ardent prohibitionists.

Rethinking harm and the role of the law

A similar allegation of naiveté may be levelled at those who campaign for fully blown legalization. Proposals for a 'market solution' have been dismissed, for example, on the basis that they are poorly thought through, politically naïve, and (worst of all) waste an opportunity to intervene positively in public policy (Dorn and South 1990). There is, in addition, no reason to suppose that legalization will eliminate all of the harms associated with illegal drugs and it is likely that there will be costs associated with such arrangements (MacCoun and Reuter 2001). Given that there is no immediate prospect of legalization, given that the notion of harmfulness justifies some form of regulation and given the apparent failure of prohibition, it is worth considering whether the notion of harm and the role of the law should be reconfigured. Of all the recent developments in criminology and criminal justice policy, it is my contention that restorative justice provides the most useful basis for such an exercise (for an overview of restorative justice see Crawford and Newburn 2003).

Restorative justice rejects the punitive orientation of the 'just deserts' model in favour of a therapeutic approach, which aims to heal hurt and injustice by encouraging participants to enter freely into a process of making amends (Braithwaite 2001). Its essential features include the following:

- crime is considered mainly to be a violation of people and their relationships, rather than a violation of the state;
- the primary focus shifts away from punishing the 'offender' onto righting wrongs and healing damaged relationships;
- reparation or making good by the 'offender' to the 'victim' is key.

Within this framework, systems of regulation that are designed in consultation with those who are to be regulated are considered superior to adversarial regulation because they limit the excuses for illegitimate means of solving frustration (Braithwaite 2001). Such systems are considered to be favourable to conventional criminal justice interventions, which rely on 'disintegrative shaming' or stigmatization and run the risk of encouraging crime by dividing the community and creating a class of outcasts. Restorative justice, by contrast, seeks to motivate the free choice to restore through a process known as 'reintegrative shaming': that is, through 'disapproval dispensed within an ongoing relationship with the offender based on respect . . . where forgiveness, apology and repentance are culturally important' (Braithwaite 1993: 1).

In practice, restorative justice seeks to turn traditional observers of the criminal justice process into active participants, typically involving 'victims' and 'perpetrators' alongside their family and friends, community volunteers and various professionals (Roche 2003). Such gatherings take various forms, including family group conferences, healing and sentencing circles, victim and offender mediation, citizens' panels and community boards. The focus is on such notions as responsibility, consequences and harm as 'victims' are given an opportunity to describe the harm they have suffered, while 'offenders' are encouraged to explain their actions and begin making amends (Braithwaite 2001).

Although restorative justice has provided an important focus for those interested in reforming the criminal justice system, it has been slow to engage with drugs issues and has had little impact in this area. It may, however, be particularly relevant because of its ability to fuse the notions of care and control. The contribution that restorative justice may make to the drugs field was recently clarified by one of its leading exponents. According to Braithwaite (2001: 229), the foundations for a restorative approach are provided by the observation that drug use can be, but is not necessarily, a source of profound injustice: 'If substance abuse[7] is part of the story of

---

7   Braithwaite (2001) was concerned with alcohol and illegal drugs.

injustice, part of what is important to understand to come to terms with the injustice, then both the substance abuse and the injustice it causes are likely to be among the things participants will wish to see healed in the restorative process'.

Restorative processes require that those who are hurt by drug use are given a chance to explain their hurts and discuss the problems they would like to see solved. They are triggered when drug use becomes serious enough to cause 'real' crime such as burglary, assault or drunk driving. Crimes that have a victim provide an opportunity for loved ones to confront the drug user's victimization of him- or herself and the collateral victimization of his or her family. In other words, a restorative strategy exploits criminalization to challenge both the harm that results from drug use and the drug use itself. At the same time, these harms are not to be treated in isolation. Restorative processes approach offences in a dynamic manner, seeking to set them in context. As a result, the wrongs that the 'offender' has done to their family and community should be considered alongside the wrongs that the community and family have committed against the 'offender'. In this way the boundaries between 'victim' and 'offender' may begin to blur (Roche 2003). Thus, for example, one of the things that participants in restorative processes may wish to see healed are the hurts and injustices that arise from attempts to punish drug use (Braithwaite 2001).[8]

An important element of Braithwaite's argument relates to the ways in which restorative justice can support rehabilitation and recovery. Being confronted with the genuine harms that result from drug use by family members and loved ones in a supportive context may help to sustain and reinforce users' motivation to change. Opportunities for making amends may also play an important role. According to the Twelve Steps programme practised by Alcoholics Anonymous and Narcotics Anonymous, for example, members 'made a list of all persons we had harmed and became willing to make amends to them all' (step eight) and 'made direct amends to such people wherever possible, except where to do so would injure them or others' (step nine) (www.alcoholics-anonymous.org, www.na.org/basic.htm). Making good in this way may help users to find a redemption narrative and create a new identity which is not based around drugs (Maruna 2001).

Conclusion

Prohibition may have largely failed as a crime-control strategy but it has been spectacularly successful as a political project. Elvins (2003) has shown how the notion of a large-scale drugs threat has been used to justify and

---

8 For examples of how restorative procedures may be used to respond to drugs issues see Roche (2003: 156–7) and Home Office (2003: 40).

legitimize extensions to the authority and control of the state, noting that almost any form of action against drug traffickers has become legitimate: in some European countries the scale of punishment for drug traffickers now exceeds that for murder. At the same time, however, there are clear signs that elements of the establishment are preparing to move in a quite different direction. The House of Commons Select Committee on Home Affairs 2002, for example, recently concluded that harm reduction rather than retribution should be the primary focus of policy towards drug users and that law enforcement should focus primarily on supply and trafficking. After almost a century, prohibition is deeply ingrained yet highly contested and only time will tell how these competing pressures play out.

References

Advisory Council on the Misuse of Drugs (ACMD) (1984) *Prevention*. London: HMSO.

Advisory Council on the Misuse of Drugs (ACMD) (2002) *The Classification of Cannabis under the Misuse of Drugs Act 1971*. London: Home Office.

Ashworth, A. (2002) Sentencing, in M. Maguire, R. Morgan and R. Reiner (eds) *The Oxford Handbook of Criminology*, 3rd edn. Oxford: Clarendon Press.

Berridge, V. (1979) Morality and medical science: concepts of narcotic addiction in Britain, 1820–1926, *Annals of Science*, 36: 67–85.

Berridge, V. and Edwards, G. (1987) *Opium and the People*, 2nd edn. New Haven, CT: Yale University Press.

Best, D., Vingoe, L. and Strang, J. (2001) *Dangerousness of Drugs*. London: National Addiction Centre/Department of Health.

Braithwaite, J. (1993) Shame and modernity, *British Journal of Criminology*, 33: 1–18.

Braithwaite, J. (2001) Restorative justice and a new criminal law of substance abuse, *Youth and Society*, 33: 227–48.

Braithwaite, J. and Pettit, L. (1990) *Not Just Deserts: A Republican Theory of Criminal Justice*. Oxford: Clarendon Press.

Crawford, A. and Newburn, T. (2003) *Youth Offending and Restorative Justice: Implementing Reform in Youth Justice*. Collumpton: Willan.

Dorn, N. and Lee, M. (1999) Drugs and policing in Europe: from low streets to high places, in N. South (ed.) *Drugs: Cultures, Controls and Everyday Life*. London: Sage.

Dorn, N. and South, N. (1990) Drug markets and law enforcement, *British Journal of Criminology*, 30: 171–88.

Downes, D. and Morgan, R. (2002) The skeletons in the cupboard: the politics of law and order at the turn of the millenium, in M. Maguire, R. Morgan and R. Reiner (eds) *The Oxford Handbook of Criminology*, 3rd edn. Oxford: Clarendon Press.

Drugscope (2004) Coke busts fail to dent price, *Druglink*, 19: 4.

Duster, T. (1970) *The Legalisation of Morality*. New York: The Free Press.

Elvins, M. (2003) *Anti-Drugs Policies of The European Union: Transnational Decision-Making and the Politics of Expertise*. Basingstoke: Palgrave Macmillan.

Home Office (2003) *Restorative Justice: the Government's Strategy*. London: Home Office.

Jay, M. (2000) *Emperors of Dreams: Drugs in the Nineteenth Century*. Sawtry: Dedalus.

Kohn, M. (1992) *Dope Girls: The Birth of the British Drug Underground*. London: Lawrence & Wishart.

Kushlick, D. (2004) The true price of prohibition, *Guardian*, 6 August.

Lacey, N. (1988) *State Punishment: Political Principles and Community Values*. London: Routledge.

Lee, M. and South, N. (2003) Drugs policing, in T. Newburn (ed.) *Handbook of Policing*. Collumpton: Willan Publishing.

MacCoun, R.J. and Reuter, P. (2001) *Drug War Heresies: Learning from Other Vices, Times and Places*. New York: Cambridge University Press.

MacGregor, S. (1999) Medicine, custom or moral fibre: policy responses to drug misuse, in N. South (ed.) *Drugs: Cultures, Controls and Everyday Life*. London: Sage.

Maruna, S. (2001) *Making Good: How Ex-Convicts Reform and Rebuild their Lives*. Washington: American Psychological Association.

Mill, J.S. (1910) *On Liberty*. London: Dent.

Newburn, T. (1992) *Permission and Regulation: Law and Morals in Post-war Britain*. London: Routledge.

Parssinen, T. (1983) *Secret Passions, Secret Remedies: Narcotic Drugs in British Society, 1820–1930*. Manchester: Manchester University Press.

Pearson, G. (1999) Drugs at the end of the century, *British Journal of Criminology*, 39: 477–87.

Police Foundation (2000) *Drugs and the Law: Report of the Independent Inquiry into the Misuse of Drugs Act 1971*. London: Police Foundation.

Roche, D. (2003) *Accountability in Restorative Justice*. Oxford: Oxford University Press.

Ruggiero, V. (1999) The legalisation of illicit substances, in N. South (ed.) *Drugs: Cultures, Controls and Everyday Life*. London: Sage.

Schur, E. (1963) *Narcotic Addiction in Britain and America*. London: Tavistock.

Schur, E. (1965) *Crimes Without Victims*. Englewood Cliffs, NJ: Prentice Hall.

Schur, E. (1969) *Our Criminal Society: The Social and Legal Sources of Crime in America*. Englewood Cliffs, NJ: Prentice Hall.

Select Committee on Home Affairs (2002) *The Government's Drugs Policy: Is it Working?* London: Stationery Office.

Smart, C. (1984) Social policy and drug addiction: a critical study of policy development, *British Journal of Addiction*, 79: 31–9.

South, N. (2002) Drugs: use, crime and control, in M. Maguire, R. Morgan and R. Reiner (eds) *The Oxford Handbook of Criminology*, 3rd edn. Oxford: Clarendon Press.

Spear, H.B. and Mott, J. (2002) *Heroin Addiction Care and Control: the British System 1916–1984*. London: Drugscope.

Trace, M., Klein, A. and Roberts, M. (2004) *Reclassification of Cannabis in the United Kingdom*. London: Drugscope/Beckley Foundation.

Travis, A. (2001) Britons Spend £6.6bn a year on drugs. Special report: drugs in Britain, *Guardian*, 22 September.

United Nations (1998) *United Nations Chronicle. XXXV*. http://www.un.org/Pubs/chronicle/ (accessed 18 March 2005).

Wilkins, L. (1965) Some sociological factors in drug addiction control, in D. Wilner and G. Kassebaum (eds) *Narcotics*. New York: McGraw-Hill.

Young, J. (1971) *The Drugtakers: The Social Meaning of Drug Use*. London: MacGibbon & Kee.

Drugs, Crime and Criminal Justice

Rhidian Hughes and Nerys Anthony

Introduction

Tensions within criminal justice policies, and between criminal justice and social welfare policies, are nowhere more apparent than when considering the issue of drugs. Large numbers of drug users are in daily contact with a range of criminal justice organizations. The police enforce laws relating to illegal drugs and the unlawful activities that surround drug use. People who are prosecuted by the Crown Prosecution Service (CPS) and found guilty by the Court Service are subject to a range of sanctions from fines or community sentences through to custody. From the outset it is important to recognize that the relationships between drugs and crime are unclear. The complex links between drugs and crime are dealt with in the first part of this chapter. This section will also review three explanatory propositions towards under-standing drugs and crime. In summary, these propositions are first that drug use leads to crime, second that crime leads to drug use, and third that crime and drug use are related to wider social forces. The policy responses aimed at tackling the drug-crime link are sketched in the second part of the chapter, where policy trends and tensions are discussed. Here the chapter provides a basic description of some of the key drug interventions within criminal justice. Concluding comments return to the premise of the chapter, that drugs and crime cannot be fully addressed through effective policies without reference to the wider social context within which they exist.

The relationships between drugs and crime

Illegal drugs are inexorably linked with crime. The international wholesale production and trafficking of drugs and the laundering of the proceeds is prohibited.[1] In the UK, the supply and possession of drugs is illegal. The following list sketches those criminal activities most commonly associated with drugs:

- acquisitive crimes motivated by drug use, such as burglary and robbery, used to pay for drugs;
- trade linked to drug use, such as street sex work;
- crimes committed under the influence of drugs, a result of the effects of drugs on the mind, including violence and anti-social behaviour; and
- crimes related to drug markets, for example turf wars and firearms offences.

Drugs and crime have common roots and are products of individuals' own actions as well as broader social structures. Heavy-end drug users, such as people who regularly use heroin and crack cocaine, undoubtedly differ from lower-end drug users. Lower-end users typically take cannabis, ecstasy and cocaine and are usually employed (Bean 2004). While harms are associated with all drugs, these lower-end users may present less threat to themselves, their communities and the state (Kalant 1999). These users have, historically, not been a policy concern, nor have policing efforts been actively targeted towards them. Recently, however, these users have entered the policy frame. With the 2005 appointment of the new Metropolitan Police Commissioner, Ian Blair, came the announcement that middle-class 'dinner party cocaine takers' would be subject to increased policing efforts (Leppard 2005). Whereas policing efforts had previously been targeted at the 'public' deals typical of 'the street', the new focus brought an emphasis on the particular spaces of restaurants, dinner parties and homes where 'elite' drugs, including cocaine, are consumed.

Like their middle-class 'dinner party' counterparts, not all individuals with heavy-end drug using behaviour are involved in criminal activity other than the purchase and supply of drugs. Some will be in paid employment, be legitimately claiming welfare benefits, or using gifts and loans to support drug use. The nexus linking drugs and crime, and one of the greatest challenges for social policy in this area, involves those individuals and groups living in socially deprived areas where drug use is an emblem of those in greatest hardship. These heavy-end drug users are typically unemployed, have experience of homelessness, are of lower social class and live in socially deprived areas. For these people, there are high financial demands on a low income, and some need large quantities of money to support their use, especially when they are drug dependent and need to use regularly. For some people, therefore, acquisitive crimes and trade linked to drug use, including sex work for some women and young men, will be used to finance drug use (as well as to fund basic life needs, including food, clothing and accommodation).

1 See, for example, www.unodc.org/unodc/en/legislation.html (accessed 8 June 2005).

Disentangling the relationships between drugs and crime raises many challenges for social research.[2] The New English and Welsh Drug Abuse Monitoring (NEW-ADAM) programme involved structured face-to-face interviews with arrestees (n = 2933) about drug use and offending and the collection of urine samples for drug testing (obtained from 95 per cent of people interviewed) in 16 police custody suites (Holloway and Bennett 2004). People get arrested for a number of different reasons and in any number of situations, and the sample is not therefore natural and nationally representative of England and Wales. It does not, for example, capture all circumstances surrounding arrest. The study is nevertheless robust enough to illustrate patterns of drugs and crime that fit trends within the broader literature (Hough 1996; Bean 2004). Some key findings from the NEW-ADAM programme include:

- *Arrestees testing positive for drugs:* drug testing of 2933 samples found 69 per cent of arrestees tested positive for one or more drugs, including cannabis, opiates, methadone, cocaine, amphetamines and benzodiazepines. Thirty-eight per cent of all samples tested positive for heroin, crack and/or cocaine.
- *Drug users and their characteristics:* 1076 (35 per cent) people interviewed were 'problem' drug users, referring to experiencing drug withdrawal when reduced amounts of drugs were consumed. Heroin dependency was reported in most (62 per cent) cases. Problem drug users were more likely to be in their twenties, white, left school at 16 or under, and received social security benefits.
- *Income:* non-drug users generated a mean illegal income of less than £6000 per year, whereas heroin, cocaine and crack users reported median illegal income in excess of £24,000.
- *Unlawful activities and self-reported connections with drugs:* Of 1655 arrestees who reported unlawful activities, 25 per cent reported committing drug supply offences. Of 1548 people who reported using any illicit drug, 60 per cent believed there was a connection between their drug use and criminal activities.

The NEW-ADAM programme illustrates some of the links between drugs and crime, but not all drug users are criminals and those drug users who commit crimes may not necessarily do so because of the drugs they consume. It is difficult to determine a sufficient (causal) connection between drug use and crime. However, there are three main explanatory propositions

---

2 For example, asking participants about unlawful activities, including criminal behaviour and drug use, is potentially 'sensitive' and may lead people to over- or under-report their actions. The relationships between drugs and crime can also be investigated differently: drug users may be asked about criminal behaviour and people in contact with criminal justice organizations might be asked about drugs.

discussed in the literature which can help to further understand the links (Seddon 2000; Bean 2004). These are:

- drug use leads to crime;
- crime leads to drug use; and
- crime and drug use are related to wider social forces.

The first proposition, that drug use leads to crime, implies that the effects of drugs on the mind and body, including the effects of increased drug tolerance, mean criminal activities are undertaken to support drug use and/or are associated with the drugs marketplace (such as firearms offences in some cases of dealing). This assertion also assumes that criminal activities, including violence, a direct result of the effects of drugs. The idea that drug use leads to crime represents the most common image presented by the media and in politics on the drugs-crime nexus. The policy implications from this understanding normally suggest that reductions in drug use, or a switching of illegal drugs to legally prescribed ones (such as prescribed methadone in place of heroin) will lead to reductions in associated criminal activity. This approach fails, however, to recognize that some drug users engage in crime prior to using drugs, that criminal activity may be related to other factors (such as 'success' in criminal undertakings), and that the prescription of substitute drugs does not necessarily lead to cessation of drug use.

The second proposition, that crime leads to drug use, originates from studies that found crime predates drug use (Burr 1987). This understanding proceeds from criminal activity that generates a disposable income that might then be used to purchase drugs, within the context of social networks in which drugs are available. The idea that crime leads to drug use suggests that drug use is an extension of criminal behaviour and associated lifestyles. These lifestyles may be supportive of risk-taking, drug use as status and as a guard against authority. Interventions need therefore to be targeted primarily towards crime. However, to do so would fail to recognize that not everyone who commits crime takes drugs (just as not all drug users commit crimes) and equally no policy can respond to all possible scenarios.

The two propositions discussed above have been developed from earlier research (see Bean 2004 for a detailed review). In contrast, the third understanding, which recognizes that drug use is influenced by a host of personal and wider social forces, is less well developed. Here, both crime and drugs are understood as complex products of individuals' circumstances and where drug use may exist together and in isolation from one another. Ethnographies highlight the complex relationships between drugs and crime as they relate to people's lives (Taylor 1993; Collison 1996). Collison (1996: xi–xii) for example points to issues of gender identity and socioeconomic structures:

For young men (and those involved in drug crime are overwhelmingly male) growing up in the de-industrialized city and structurally excluded from the world of work (and one major source of masculine identity), and perennially on the margins of education, organized leisure, the family and citizenship in general, the drug economy can be central to both their material and symbolic lives. Drug use and drug distribution generate local cultural role models inflected by global images (relayed through media communication) which signify the centrality of drugs to daily life, opportunity, status and liberative experience (via risk from anxiety or the simple boredom of modern forms of reason).

Bean (2004) identifies a number of sub-models within which drug use is related to a wider social forces model. Here drugs and crime are argued to:

- have common origins;
- be reciprocally related;
- occur simultaneously; and
- be shaped by policy.

Understanding that drugs and crime have common origins and/or occur simultaneously suggests that the causes of drug use and crime need first to be tackled. The reciprocal relationship sub-model is similar to the drugs causes crime model, and is equally limited. The effect of policy in shaping drug use and crime is largely unexplored but combined with an appreciation of the common origins and simultaneous occurrence of drug use and crime may offer a more complete, ideal type, explanation. This has significant implications for the ability of current drug policies to have the intended impact.

Drugs and criminal justice: a sketch of trends and some policy tensions

From the 1920s (and the Rolleston 1926 Committee report) through to the early 1970s, explanations for drug use (primarily heroin use) focused on drug users' pathologies. Psychiatric and medical approaches dominated policy responses to drugs and crime. Reductions in drug use through treatment were seen as satisfactory outcomes (Advisory Council on the Misuse of Drugs 1982), and increased emphasis was placed on law enforcement for those not in treatment and/or involved in crime (Home Office 1985).

The emergence of human immunodeficiency virus (HIV), and the perceived threat to individuals and communities, as a public health issue, led to a refocusing of drug policies. Harm reduction approaches became important because they recognized drug users may not necessarily halt drug use. Reducing the spread of infection through needle exchange schemes, for example, was regarded as more important for drug users and society than halting the consumption of drugs *per se*. As Hart (1990: 138) notes, this was 'an example of government stomaching one "evil" . . . in order to obviate others'. This harm reduction approach broadly characterized policy until the early 1990s.[3]

In 1993, significant changes to policy responses to drug use in society, and crime in particular, occurred. At the Conservative Party conference in 1993 Michael Howard, then Home Secretary, introduced a 'law and order' proposal package, which included substantial revisions to current practice working with drug users, and in so doing impeded the emphasis on harm reduction. For the first time also, prisons were targeted in a 'crackdown' on drug use, when Howard gave his 'prison works' speech. The emphasis on drug use in prisons emerged from feelings regarding 'soft' prison conditions and high levels of drug-taking. A year later the government Green Paper reflected the political agenda with a new national drug strategy placing increased controls on drug use (Her Majesty's Government 1994). In 1995 the White Paper was published with a retreat from the harm reduction focus of the 1980s (Her Majesty's Government 1995).

The 1995 White Paper, *Tackling Drugs Together*, introduced key performance indicators upon which progress would be measured (HM Government 1995). The drive towards performance indicators in the drugs field occurred within a broader public policy context of making public services auditable (Power 1997). Bean (2004) notes that during the early 1990s, interest in economic models for drugs and crime increased and economic market models heavily influenced policy-making. Economic market models emphasize the importance of drug prices as a factor influencing consumption[4] with price being a key determinant of entry into treatment (when drugs cannot be afforded, people enter treatment).

The New Labour government maintained the policy profile introduced in the 1995 White Paper but did so within the context of aspirations to reduce drug use and crime to 'protect communities'. In 1998, the government launched its ten-year drug strategy (Her Majesty's Government 1998). It intensified the 'managerial' approach towards drug policy and the use of key performance indicators. One of the key aims was to reduce the effects of drug use on the community, including criminal behaviour. Reducing repeat offending by drug users was emphasized as a key objective as well as the cost effectiveness of treatment.[5] An update to the national drug strategy (Home Office 2002a) was published alongside a specific plan to tackle

---

3 See Berridge (1996) and Stimson (1995) for detailed policy analysis of responses to HIV.
4 The lower the price the more drugs are consumed and vice versa.
5 One of the key drivers for this shift in agendas was research pointing to the economic costs of drug use and the cost efficiencies to be achieved through treatment. The emphasis is that treatment works and is cost effective. It is pointed out that for every £1 spent on treatment, at least £3 is saved in terms of reduced 'victim' costs of crime and demands on the criminal justice system (Gossop *et al.* 2001).

crack supply and use (Home Office 2002b).[6] The drug strategies and updates over the last decade assume clear links between drug use and crime and have combined to shape criminal justice responsibilities for, and practice towards, drugs and drug users. Explicit within government strategies is a continuing emphasis of a particular understanding of drugs-crime links, notably that acquisitive crimes are committed by (predominantly heavy-end) drug users. Introducing the updated drug strategy the then Home Secretary, David Blunkett wrote:

> The use of drugs contributes dramatically to the volume of crime as users take cash and possessions from others in a desperate attempt to raise the money to pay the dealers. In addition, otherwise decent people become dealers in pyramid selling, as they persuade friends, acquaintances and strangers to take on the habit, so that they themselves can fund their own addiction.
>
> (Home Office 2002a: 3)

This current view is based on the assumption that drug use leads to crime. It does not, therefore, appreciate the wider dynamics underpinning drug use and criminal activity, nor how the two are influenced by wider social forces.

The biggest shift since the harm reduction approach to drug use in the 1980s concerns the ways in which drug treatment has been developed since 1997. The implementation of drug treatment policies was designed to reduce crime rather than to tackle drug use as a health and social welfare issue (Stimson 2000; Hunt and Stevens 2004). Thus, criminal justice has become the main gateway to drug treatment. A range of criminal justice structures are now in place towards addressing drug use. An illustration of drug interventions within current criminal justice structures is given in Figure 6.1. A basic description of key drug interventions is given in Box 6.1.

One of the core developments in tackling drugs and crime has been the introduction of enhanced treatment options within the criminal justice system, including Drug Treatment and Testing Orders (DTTOs). DTTOs were introduced in 2000 as a new community sentence as an alternative to custody under the Crime and Disorder Act 1998. A change in legislation with the Criminal Justice Act 2003, introduced in April 2005, has seen the traditional DTTO renamed with its core components (drug testing and drug treatment) included as an option for sentencers within the Drug Rehabilitation Requirement (DRR). The principles remain the same, however, in that community sentences are designed for problematic drug users who commit criminal activities to fund drug use and express a desire to

---

6 The crack plan was prompted by particularly high levels of crime among crack users and 'high crack areas' were identified for targeted intervention. Addressing crack use is part of a broader recognition of drug treatment services being primarily opiate focused and crack users' needs being left unaddressed (Strang and Gossop 1994).

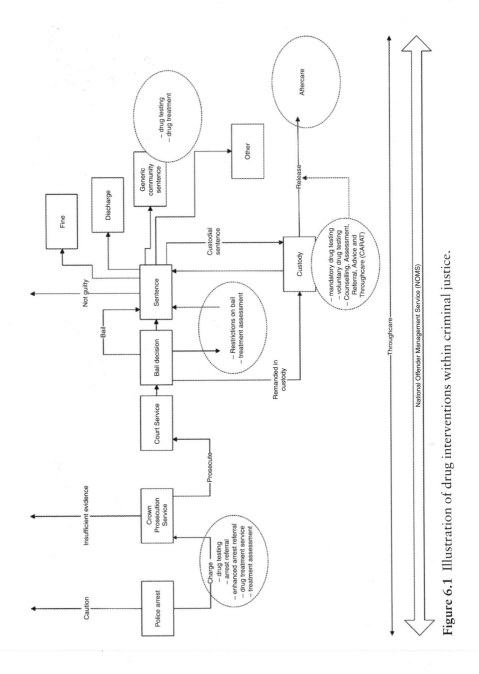

Figure 6.1 Illustration of drug interventions within criminal justice.

Box 6.1 The Organisation and Structure of Criminal Justice Services: a Basic Description

An individual using drugs may take any number of routes through the criminal justice system. During this time their drug use may or may not be detected and acted upon (therefore determining whether suitable treatment is identified, accessed and provided).

The Drug Intervention Programme (DIP)[7] was introduced in 'high crime areas' during April 2003 and rolled out across England and later in Wales. The programme is primarily focused on reducing drug-related crime, and comprises local interventions to detect drug use, 'divert' people into treatment and reduce crime. The expectation is to reduce offending.

Drug interventions: police custody

During the course of police arrest, caution, charge, detention and release within police stations a number of drug interventions are available.

Pre-arrest schemes employ proactive police disruption and targeting to identify and encourage drug-using offenders to access treatment and other support. Deferred cautioning in some areas includes the opportunity to engage in treatment as a condition of caution and on the understanding that the criminal activity will stop.

Arrest referral and enhanced arrest referral schemes involve drug treatment workers in police custody suites assessing and referring individuals into treatment. The workers may 'case manage' drug users, including devising care plans and providing low level treatment interventions.[8] At this stage treatment assessment will also be made.

Detainees charged with 'trigger' offences – including theft, robbery, burglary, deception, handling stolen goods, taking without consent, begging and the production and supply of drugs – may be drug tested within police custody suites. Where an individual tests positive they are encouraged to meet with an arrest referral worker with a view to identifying and addressing their treatment needs. The result of the drug test will be made available to the court and can be used to assist in bail decision-making and sentencing.

Drug intervention: restrictions on bail

Restrictions on bail, as a drug intervention, were introduced in May 2004. Bail restrictions can be placed on people tested positive for drugs within police custody. The court can order an individual to undergo a drug assessment and agree to any treatment as part of bail conditions. Where an individual agrees they will be granted conditional bail, however where they refuse, bail is not granted. This intervention therefore reduces the circumstances in which bail can be presumed.[9]

---

7 Formally known as Criminal Justice Interventions Programme (CJIP).
8 See Sondhi *et al.* (2003) for further details.
9 See Home Office (2004) for details.

Drug interventions: community sentencing

Generic community sentencing can include specific interventions directed at people using drugs. These interventions include drug testing and drug treatment, which may or may not be used together, forming the Drug Rehabilitation Requirement. The delivery of community sentences by local probation areas, under the remit of 'supervision', may include accredited programmes directed at addressing drug use, such as Addressing Substance Related Offending (ASRO) and Offender Substance Abuse Drug Interventions Programme (OSAP). Such programmes may be delivered by probation teams or other commissioned providers in group work settings.

Drug interventions: imprisonment

A range of interventions exist within prisons to address drug use. All prisons have the Counselling, Assessment, Referral, Advice and Throughcare (CARAT) service available to prisoners where low-level support is provided to meet individuals' needs. Some prisons may operate 'enhanced' CARAT schemes providing intense support.

Other prison based drug interventions include:

- mandatory drug testing, periodically undertaken across all prisons on a random sample of prisoners;
- voluntary drug testing, available on a voluntary basis for prisoners;
- residential detoxification facilities, provided for the clinical management of drug withdrawal; and
- rehabilitation programmes and therapeutic communities, for some individuals identified as in need of such an intervention.

Aftercare

Aftercare is part of the DIP programme whereby those leaving prison with an identified drug-related problem are supported by drug treatment workers based in the community. Aftercare workers seek to ensure that appropriate drug treatment is in place for an individual immediately on release from prison. Aftercare can also include support with wider issues, for example housing, relationships, education and employment.

Throughcare

Throughcare is a key component of the DIP programme. This involves continual support to drug users from arrest through to sentence. Specific teams within DIP operate case management to support individuals at all stages of the process.

Prolific and other Priority Offenders (PPOs) strategy

2004 saw the launch of the PPO strategy which targets offenders that are responsible for the highest number of crimes nationally (this constitutes 5000 offenders that undertake one in ten offences). Where PPOs are drug users they will be offered treatment or arrest and subsequently fast tracked to court.

National Offender Management Service (NOMS)

The NOMS was established in 2004. It aims to supervise offenders through an integrated approach focusing on 'end-to-end management'. It seeks to deliver this approach through the joining of prison and probation into correctional services. The NOMS will also introduce contestability into criminal justice, by establishing a 'marketplace' within which services for offenders, and offending drug users, will be commissioned and delivered. The management and treatment of problematic drug users within the correctional services has been identified as a priority.

stop taking drugs. However, under the DRR an individual may be ordered to undergo drug testing without treatment, or vice versa. Individuals are likely to be given close supervision and counselling from dedicated teams and a range of welfare professionals, including health, housing and employment. People tested for drug use may undergo treatment and attend court review hearings. The effectiveness of DTTOs is geographically variable however, with high levels of order revocations and reconvictions, which highlights the importance of timely support services noted to be inadequate or missing (Hough *et al.* 2003). In some areas DTTOs have been rationed and sentencers are unable to make full use of the provisions (Her Majesty's Chief Inspector of Constabulary *et al.* 2003). Testing without treatment may 'set offenders up to fail' and may therefore lead to low uptake by sentencers (Matrix Research and Consultancy and NACRO 2004).

The balancing of health care functions and criminal justice control functions raises important issues for social policy. The current state of policy is that in some situations there may be a perverse incentive to engage in criminal activities to access drug treatment particularly where rapid prescribing is available within DIP. Furthermore, Turning Point (2003) report a lack of resources for community drug treatment which results in long waiting times for some drug users, which can negatively affect people's motivation to seek help if services cannot be accessed immediately. Overly advantageous 'fast track' treatment, such as that which DTTOs/DRR/DIP provide, might also 'reward' people for offending by giving them better treatment options than drug users accessing support in the community. A participant in Turning Point's (2003: 31) consultation, for example, remarked, 'On a DTTO, it takes three days to get a script. Without a DTTO it takes four months'. Reflecting geographical inequities in DTTO provision, in some areas, the situation has led some local authorities to request drug treatment within prisons for drug users in the community (Her Majesty's Chief Inspector of Constabulary *et al.* 2003). The Home Affairs Select Committee (2002:

para. 262) has addressed these concerns and made recommendations to government: 'We consider it highly undesirable that it should be easier for a drug addict to access treatment through the criminal justice system than in the community. This is a further reason, if any were needed, for the Government to provide more treatment in the community'.

Concern about treatment has grown to such an extent that the Sentencing Guidelines Council has been called upon to provide guidance to sentencers to ensure that drug users are not sent to prison solely because it offers a more favourable ground for treatment than can be provided in the community (Esmée Fairbairn Foundation 2004). Just as there are concerns regarding the ways in which people might access criminal justice services to receive treatment, there are concerns as to the impact of treatment in a criminal justice context should (or realistically, when) some individuals relapse. Breach of treatment orders can result in further criminal proceedings, including custodial sentences. In addition to DTTOs/DRR, for example, criminal justice agencies, including the police, have stronger powers to require people to attend treatment. The 2005 Drugs Act gives the police powers to drug test those arrested for 'trigger' offences, but not charged or found guilty of an offence. The police can also require, along with treatment staff, those who test positive to attend drug assessment and follow-up assessments, with treatment plans. Drug workers must inform the police when treatment plans are broken and this can result in fines or imprisonment (Home Office 2005). Any refusal may lead to fines or up to three years in prison. The Transform Drug Policy Foundation (2005) raise a number of human rights concerns with the provisions. For example, they argue that a net-widening precedent has been set and the next step might be to drug test people stopped and searched. Should people mistakenly arrested refuse to undergo a drug test they will be criminalized and could be fined and/or imprisoned. Furthermore: 'It seems disingenuous for the Home Office to describe the testing requirements as "*not onerous*" when they are backed up by the threat of imprisonment, a threat that is further more described as making it "*easier for the drug misuser to comply*" ' (Transform Drug Policy Foundation 2005: 13).

In addition to these concerns by the Transform Drug Policy Foundation, the likelihood of these drug-testing measures being successful is limited given the findings from previous research (Hough *et al.* 2003; Matrix Research and Consultancy and NACRO 2004; Holloway *et al.* 2005). Matrix Research and Consultancy and NACRO (2004) evaluated drug testing of people charged with trigger offences[10] within police stations, during pre-

---

10 Trigger offences include theft, robbery, burglary, deception, handling stolen goods, taking without consent, begging and the production and supply of drugs as specified under the Theft Act 1968 and Misuse of Drugs Act 1971.

sentence, as part of a Drug Abstinence Order, Drug Abstinence Requirement or drug testing when on licence or under a Notice of Supervision. The evaluation found that drug testing alone did not reduce drug consumption or criminal behaviour. However, when drug testing was undertaken as part of a community sentence or licence condition following release, better outcomes in terms of reductions in drug use and crime were achieved along with individuals' increased engagement with the treatment process. This was achieved through motivational interviewing techniques and access to wider supportive interventions, for example helping people with housing. The key policy implication of the results of the Matrix Research and Consultancy and NACRO (2004) evaluation was that drug testing alone will not reduce drug use or criminal behaviour. Findings from a systematic review of interventions to reduce drug-related crime support the importance of intensive supervision and the review concludes that 'there is no clear evidence that routine monitoring drug testing works' (Holloway *et al.* 2005: v). The fact that the drug testing pilot programme was rolled out before the research was completed reflects somewhat on the government's strong push towards drug testing despite the lack of evidence of effectiveness.

Carlen (1996) argues that two dominant discourses have repeatedly surrounded the treatment of vulnerable groups in social policy. These discourses – citizen risk and less eligibility – date back to the historical roots of social policy and enshrine the view that those who pose a risk to society are less eligible for social welfare or eligible only in prescribed circumstances when deemed to have benefits for the wider community. Drug users cause a risk to society and are, therefore, treated in ways that make them less eligible for welfare. With the exception of some mental health care provisions, in no other area of health policy is the direct provision of care linked to i) coercion and ii) criminal justice. The current focus towards drug users, and other vulnerable groups, reflects broader characteristics of society: a culture of individualism with decreasing concerns about inequalities and poverty coupled with increasingly Draconian attitudes to offenders (Foster 2000). This is a result of the increased politicization of law and order policy agendas. The situation means that highly visible unlawful activities (usually a product of political and media attention) are subject to attention and blaming, whereas others are subject to none.

> We do not seem to be concerned with all crimes against the criminal law, and are not bothered about "middle class" crime, for example, fiddling expenses or taxes. Why are some "thefts" not considered to be crime, for example, the work "sicky" or misuse of computers at work, or are dealt with as largely civil offences? . . . Our concerns are about volume, visibility, violence and abuse against the person or personal theft; but we are not so worried about concerns against "anonymous" institutions or systems. That means it is the visible poor, the underclass,

the excluded, who remain the victims and the focus of legislation, the law and the criminal justice system.

(Grieve and Howard 2004: 6)

Concluding comments

The issue of drugs, crime and criminal justice has been subject to much attention in recent years. Policy focus has tinkered at the edges of some complex social issues surrounding drugs and criminal justice but little has been done to seriously challenge or shift prevailing views and approaches towards drug users and/or those in contact with criminal justice. The expectation among policy-makers is that drug users should become abstinent when given opportunities to access treatment and that these reductions in drug use will reduce crime. Drug treatment is therefore provided as a criminal justice function and it seems likely that the current trend will remain the same for the foreseeable future.

As noted earlier, the links between drugs and crime are more complex than the logic of current policy (drugs lead to crime) would suggest. Wider social forces continue to influence and shape the lives of disadvantaged and vulnerable groups and communities. Drugs and crime exist within deeply embedded social and cultural systems of social deprivation, and it is this nettle – of social inequalities – that is hard for policy-makers to grasp. In an era where urine tests and saliva swabs lead performance management, and in turn drugs policy, it is difficult to imagine holistic policy responses towards drugs. Within the current policy climate, performance management focuses attention on the process and immediate outputs of interventions (e.g. numbers immediately accessing treatment) rather than the longer-term outcomes (such as behavioural change maintained over time).

To focus on these longer-term outcomes requires wider social issues that are closely linked with drugs and crime to be addressed. The neglect of these wider social factors remains at the heart of calls for improved drugs and crime policy-making. NACRO (2003: 15) argues that policies must be shaped humanely and to be effective '[need] to be tough on the causes of drugs'. Turning Point (2003: 7) call for drug policy performance measures in treatment to be based on social causes of drugs, and specifically: 'The success of drug treatment, whether provided in the community or via the criminal justice system, should be measured against a new target to reduce deprivation and promote social inclusion'.

Policy needs a rethink. Clearly, policy-makers should target their efforts on the social forces that enable drugs and crime to exist. The challenge is integrating the cross-cutting policy areas that surround drugs and crime to produce those much sought-after 'joined up' approaches that are little understood and difficult to achieve (Roche 2004). This can mean any number of different things in any number of policy arenas. As a flavour it can be taken to include, and join up, support for families where drug use is a source of stress, constructive educational, employment or leisure programmes to young people at risk and recognizing when people are in contact with criminal justice that a 'one size fits all' approach towards drugs, including abstinence, does not work. Also required is an acceptance of contradictions inherent in formulating social policy regarding drugs. This acceptance should recognize that drug use and crime will continue to exist, yet tackling the social causes will yield more effective societal-level responses to drug use than punitive approaches to drug-taking as currently employed.

References

Advisory Council on the Misuse of Drugs (1982) *Treatment and Rehabilitation*. London: HMSO.

Bean, P. (2004) *Drugs and Crime*. Collompton: Willan.

Berridge, V. (1996) *AIDS in the UK: The Making of Policy, 1981–1994*. Oxford: Oxford University Press.

Burr, A. (1987) Chasing the dragon: heroin misuse, delinquency and crime in the context of south London culture, *British Journal of Criminology*, 27: 333–57.

Carlen, P. (1996) *Jigsaw – A Political Criminology of Youth Homelessness*. Buckingham: Open University Press.

Collison, M. (1996) *Police, Drugs and Community*. London: Free Association Books.

Esmée Fairbairn Foundation (2004) *Rethinking Crime & Punishment: The Report*. London: Esmée Fairbairn Foundation.

Foster, J. (2000) Social exclusion, crime and drugs, *Drugs: Education, Prevention and Policy*, 7: 317–30.

Gossop, M., Marsden, J. and Duncan, S. (2001) *NTORS After Five Years: The National Treatment Outcome Research Study: Changes in Substance use, Health and Criminal Behaviour During the Five Years after Intake*. London: National Addiction Centre.

Grieve, J. and Howard, R. (2004) Introduction, in J. Grive and R. Howard (eds) *Communities, Social Exclusion and Crime*. London: Smith Institute.

Hart, G. (1990) Needle exchange in historical context: responses to the 'drugs problem', in P. Aggleton, P. Davies and G. Hart (eds) *AIDS: Individual, Cultural and Policy Dimensions*. London: Falmer Press.

Her Majesty's Government (1994) *Tackling Drugs Together: A Strategy for England 1995–1998*. London: Stationery Office.

Her Majesty's Government (1998) *Tackling Drugs to Build a Better Britain: The Government's Ten Year Strategy for Tackling Drug Misuse*. London: Stationery Office.

Her Majesty's Chief Inspector of Constabulary, Chief Inspector of Social Services, Her Majesty's Chief Inspector of the Crown Prosecution Service, Her Majesty's Chief Inspector of the Magistrates Courts Services and Her Majesty's Chief

Inspector of Probation (2003) *Streets Ahead: A Joint Inspection of the Street Crime Initiative*. London: Home Office.

Holloway, K. and Bennett, T. (2004) *The Results of the First Two Years of the NEW-ADAM Programme*. Home Office Online Report 19/04, www.homeoffice.gov.uk/rds/pdfs04/rdsolr1904.pdf (accessed 31 May 2005).

Holloway, K., Bennett, T. and Farrington, D. (2005) *The Effectiveness of Criminal Justice and Treatment in Reducing Drug-Related Crime: A Systematic Review*. Home Office Online Report 26/05, www.homeoffice.gov.uk/rds/drugs1.html (accessed 31 May 2005).

Home Affairs Select Committee (2002) *The Government's Drug Policy: Is it Working?* Third report.

Home Office (1985) *Tackling Drug Misuse*. London: HMSO.

Home Office (2002a) *Updated Drug Strategy 2002*. London: Home Office.

Home Office (2002b) *Tackling Crack: A National Plan*. London: Home Office.

Home Office (2004) *Criminal Justice Act 2003. Drug Users: Restriction on Bail (Pilots)*. London: Home Office.

Home Office (2005) *Drugs Bill Receives Royal Assent*. London: Home Office.

Hough, M. (1996) *Drug Misuse and the Criminal Justice System: A Review of the Literature*. London: Home Office.

Hough, M., Clancy, A., McSweeney, T. and Turnbull, P.J. (2003) *The Impact of Drug Treatment and Testing Orders on Offending: Two Year Reconviction Results*. London: Home Office.

Hunt, N. and Stevens, A. (2004) Whose harm? Harm reduction and the shift to coercion in UK drug policy, *Social Policy and Society*, 3: 333–42.

Kalant, H. (1999) Differentiating drugs by harm potential: the rational versus the feasible, *Substance Use & Misuse*, 34: 25–34.

Leppard, D. (2005) Secret policemen to sniff out dinner party cocaine takers, *Sunday Times*, 6 February.

Matrix Research and Consultancy and NACRO (2004) *Evaluation of Drug Testing in the Criminal Justice System*. London: Home Office.

NACRO (2003) *Drugs and Crime: From Warfare to Welfare*. London: NACRO.

Power, M. (1997) *The Audit Society, Rituals of Verification*. Oxford: Clarendon Press.

Roche, M. (2004) Complicated problems, complicated solutions? Homelessness and joined up policy responses, *Social Policy & Administration*, 38: 758–74.

Rolleston, H. (1926) *Report on the Committee on Morphine and Heroin Addiction*. London: Ministry of Health.

Seddon, T. (2000) Explaining the drug-crime link: theoretical, policy and research issues, *Journal of Social Policy*, 29: 95–107.

Sondhi, A., O'Shea, J. and Williams, T. (2003) *Arrest Referral: Emerging Findings from the National Monitoring and Evaluation Programme*. London: Home Office.

Stimson, G.V. (1995) AIDS and injecting drug use in the United Kingdom 1987–1993: the policy response and the prevention of the epidemic, *Social Science and Medicine*, 41: 699–716.

Stimson, G.V. (2000) 'Blair declares war': the unhealthy state of British drug policy, *International Journal of Drug Policy*, 11: 259–64.

Strang, J. and Gossop, M. (1994) *Heroin Addiction and Drug Policy: The British System*. Oxford: Oxford University Press.

Taylor, A. (1993) *Women Drug Users: An Ethnography of a Female Injecting Community*. Oxford: Oxford University Press.

Transform Drug Policy Foundation (2005) *Response to the Drugs Bill 2005*. Second reading briefing. Bristol: Transform Drug Policy Foundation.

Turning Point (2003) *Routes into Treatment: Drugs and Crime*. London: Turning Point.

Further reading

Bean, P. (2004) *Drugs and Crime*. Collompton: Willan.

Blunkett, D. (2004) *Reducing Crime – Changing Lives. The Government's Plans for Transforming the Management of Offenders*. London: Home Office.

Davies, M., Croall, H. and Tyrer, J. (2005) *Criminal Justice: An Introduction to the Criminal Justice System in England and Wales*. London: Pearson.

NACRO (2003) *Drugs and Crime: From Warfare to Welfare*. London: NACRO.

Turning Point (2003) *Routes into Treatment: Drugs and Crime*. London: Turning Point.

chapter

seven

Drugs and Health Policy

Rachel Lart

Introduction

In March 2000 one of the leading academics in the drugs field, Gerry Stimson, launched a fierce attack on the direction and content of British drugs policy under the Blair Labour government. The main thrust of his critique was that since 1997, there had been a switch from a 'healthy drugs policy' to an 'unhealthy' one, characterized by the conflation of drug use with crime, the drug user with criminality and the co-option of treatment as a means of tackling crime. This he contrasted with the previous ten years (1987–97) of policy, which had seen a public health approach and the development of harm reduction measures, with the drug user's own health and their ability to lead a healthier life as the focus of intervention (Stimson 2000).

This chapter explores the relationship between drugs policy and health policy. Commentators have differed in the balance they see between, and the significance they give to, the roles of health/medical agencies and policies on the one hand, and enforcement and criminal justice agencies and policies on the other, in British drugs policy. In particular, commentators from North America have often argued that in Britain the use of illicit drugs has been understood primarily as a health-related or medical issue and that the drug user was seen as a misfortunate who was 'sick' in some way (Schur 1961, 1963; Lindesmith 1972; Trebach 1982). This has been selected, usually with approval, as distinguishing British from US policy. As Dorn and South argue 'in this vision, the criminal law was variously seen as absent, as epiphenomenal or as an irrational distraction from treatment' (1994: 293). In reality, the 'big' framework of British policy has always, since the early twentieth century, been that of the criminal law and the lead government department, the Home Office (Berridge 1984; Stimson and Lart 1994). The exertion of that overall control has been more or less overt at different times in the history of policy, and within that framework the medical/health response has been a key part of policy. It is with this that this chapter is concerned.

What I will argue is that drugs policy cannot be seen in isolation from the norms and frameworks of broader health policy. The early part of the century and the first decades of the National Health Service (NHS) were the era of medical freedom and professional autonomy, while the 1970s and 1980s saw the development of central planning and coordination between tiers of the health service, and the development of intersectoral and multi-agency working. This last characteristic has developed even more in the last 10–15 years, with the notion of 'joined-up working' becoming central to New Labour social policies. Drugs are one of the 'wicked issues' (Rittel and Webber 1973) which cross sectoral boundaries, and for which there are no universally agreed definitions and desired outcomes, yet by their nature demand joint working between social policy fields.

Another key part of the current health policy landscape is the development of centralized mechanisms to ensure effective and equitable provision of services. In the broader health policy field this has taken the form of the creation of the National Institute for Clinical Excellence (NICE) and the development of guidelines and protocols for specific treatments and procedures along with systems of clinical governance to ensure individual practice is in line with these. In specific policy fields, National Service Frameworks (NSFs) have been developed and the drugs field is one of these, with the document *Models of Care* (NTA 2002). All these developments are based on changing definitions of good practice, and how good practice is determined. This means a change from the collective opinion of the 'great and the good' expressed through various forms such as Royal Commissions, advisory committees and professional bodies, to evidence-based practice based on the rigorous scrutiny and evaluation of alternative interventions.

Key themes in this chapter are: the changing nature of the relationship between professionals and the state; the development of coordinating structures across sectors and between levels of government; and the significance of evidence-based practice within the drugs field. The period concentrated on is from the early 1980s, encompassing the two phases of policy that Stimson was describing. However, some analysis of earlier policy is needed and so I start with a discussion of the first part of the twentieth century, the period generally described as being typified by the 'British System' of drug treatment.

The British System of drug treatment

This chapter does not describe in detail the earlier history of British drugs policy. Good accounts and analyses of this can be found elsewhere. The nineteenth century is well covered in Berridge and Edwards (1987), Berridge and Edwards (1998), Jay (2000), Holloway (1995), Davenport-Hines (2002) and Harding (1988, 1998). The most significant point for this chapter is that in the late nineteenth century, a growing concern about the effects on the working-class population of drug use, especially opiate use, led to public health-type controls, focusing on the point of sale. The 1868 Pharmacy Act brought the retail of opiates under professional pharmaceutical control and was to some extent successful in reducing popular consumption (Berridge and Edwards 1987). The medical *treatment* of those experiencing problems as a result of addiction, however, remained a matter of professional discretion, within the traditions of privatized and individualized practice.

During the First World War, concerns about cocaine consumption by servicemen led to action under the Defence of the Realm Act to control access to cocaine. This made it an offence to be in possession of cocaine without a prescription (Spear 1994). After the war, and at least partly because of pressures from international treaties, the wartime controls were extended under the Dangerous Drugs Act 1920 to cover morphine and heroin. This raised the issue of what was good medical practice in prescribing for the treatment of addiction. The Rolleston Committee was set up to consider this issue, and its report, in 1926, formed the backbone of policy for the next 40 years – what became known as the 'British System' of drug treatment and policy. The 'British System' is discussed in Berridge (1980, 1984), Berridge and Edwards (1998), Lart (1998), Mott and Bean (1998) and South (1998).

What is key to understanding the relationship between drugs policy and health policy is that the British System was not really a system, but a reflection of a particular understanding of the relationship between the medical profession and the state, and between the individual doctor and the patient (Spear 1994; Stimson and Lart 1994). The British System did not dictate the nature of treatment, but allowed individual medical practitioners to choose what they saw as appropriate treatment, including the possibility of long-term prescribing, what would later be termed 'maintenance' prescribing, for their patients. This choice was placed within a framework of legal control and oversight, but remained an issue of individualized medical practice. This individual right to practice as one saw fit remained central to British health policy, even after the advent of the NHS in 1948. Indeed, allowing clinicians professional and individual autonomy over what constituted good practice was central to the accommodation made by Aneurin Bevan with the medical profession in order to create the NHS (Bevan 1952; Klein 1995).

This low-key way of dealing with drug users was acceptable so long as the users themselves were not perceived as a social threat in any way. In the 1960s, the growth in numbers of young people using heroin recreationally raised the question of whether the Rolleston-based system of prescribing and, in particular, the role of general practitioners prescribing, was still appropriate. The second Brain Report (Interdepartmental Committee on

Drug Addiction 1965) reflected a change in the medical model of addiction from an individualized and somatic disease, appropriately treated by GPs, to a psychiatric condition which was socially contagious (Lart 1998). This new conceptualization made heroin addiction a 'menace to society' (Inter-departmental Committee on Drug Addiction 1965: para. 18) and led to the policy recommendations of a restriction on prescribing, the establishment of specialist treatment centres and the creation of a system of notification (Strang and Gossop 1994). The Ministry of Health guidelines enacting these recommendations made explicit the dual role of treatment – care of the individual and control of the social problem of addiction (Connell and Strang 2005). The most significant change was the imposition under the Dangerous Drugs Act 1967 (and the subsequent Misuse of Drugs Act 1971) of limits on the right of most doctors to prescribe heroin and some other opiates, and cocaine, for the treatment of addiction. This became restricted to doctors holding a licence from the Home Office. In practice this was largely the consultant psychiatrists running the new Drug Dependency Clinics. This change did not mean a fundamental change in the overall legis-lative framework for the control of drugs – it was a change in what that framework allowed the medical profession to do. As such, neither was it a change imposed on the profession by a repressive Home Office. Bing Spear, the Home Office Chief Inspector at the time, reports that the Home Office would have been satisfied with a system of self-regulation by the profession – something that Rolleston had intended but which had never in fact been enacted (Trebach 1982; *BJA* 1988). The shape of drugs policy which emerged after the second Brain Report was largely a result of discussion and proposals from within the medical profession, and was aimed at controlling the GPs who were blamed for fuelling the epidemic of heroin use through prescribing practices (Fazey 1979; Smart 1984; Connell and Strang 1994; Lart 1998). The treatment of addiction was now defined as a task for psychiatry as a specialism and largely carried on in hospital settings, albeit mainly on an outpatient basis.

The 1970s saw the consolidation of the psychiatric model for treating addiction, and a move away from the role of social control. In the early days, the necessity of prescribing injectable heroin was accepted, albeit reluctantly, by most of the staff of the clinics, as a means of 'undercutting the black market' and stabilizing what was seen as a social problem. This changed over the ensuing decade and prescribing practice shifted away from heroin to the substitute drug methadone, and from the injectable form of this to oral preparations. Again, this shift in practice was not something imposed on the profession by the Home Office, but emerged from the profession's own definitions of good practice and informal systems of peer review (Mitchison 1994). The goal of the clinics became the cure of the individual addict, and not the control of a social menace (Lart 1998; Connell and Strang 2005; Strang *et al.* 2005). The numbers of people on the Home

Office Index (now backed up by a formal system of notification) continued to rise throughout the 1970s, almost doubling from 2657 in 1970 to 5107 in 1980 (Mott 1994). However, the sense of crisis and of an epidemic had passed.

The 1980s epidemic and response

The 1980s have been overshadowed by the emergence of HIV transmission among injecting drug users, and of the response in British drugs policy to this – the development of the philosophy of harm minimization or reduction, and practices such as needle and syringe exchange (O'Hare *et al.* 1992; Stimson 1994). However, it is important to understand changes that occurred in both the underlying conceptualization of drug use as an issue and in the pattern of services, prior to the advent of HIV, in order to see how these could be the response to the disease. Other countries, notably the USA and Sweden, did not adopt the measures Britain did and elsewhere change was slower, indicating that there was nothing inevitable about harm minimization as a response to the perceived crisis of HIV transmission.

In the early 1980s a new 'heroin epidemic' emerged, with very different features from that of the 1960s. Between 1980 and 1985, the average yearly increase in notifications was 30 per cent, with a single increase of 50 per cent in new notifications recorded for 1983. By 1985, the total number of people on the Index was 14,688 (Mott 1994), with almost all new notifications that year being users of heroin (as opposed to methadone or other drugs). The key to the importance of this was not just the numbers but the changes in the patterns of drug use that the Index suggested.

One aspect of this was changes in the sources of notifications. The proportion of new notifications coming from GPs rose. A survey carried out in 1985 suggested that in any given four-week period, a fifth of all GPs in England and Wales saw at least one opiate user, and that GPs as a whole saw 40,000 cases over a 12-month period (Glanz and Taylor 1986). Another aspect was age. People under the age of 21 increased to 24 per cent of all notifications in 1985, compared to 17 per cent in 1979. The significance of this is not so much the numbers in this age group, but that the rise reversed the trends of the 1970s. It indicated that young people were continuing to start using notifiable drugs, rather than there being a cohort of people using drugs who were steadily growing older. Both these factors, age and source of notification, suggested that, far from being contained by the specialist psychiatrically-based drugs services, illicit drug use was becoming a more widespread phenomenon.

The epidemic was geographically diffused. Historically drug use had been seen very much as centred on London and a few other major cities. A feature of the epidemic of the 1980s was the geographic spread involved. While

London may have remained the 'centre of gravity' (Pearson 1987: 5), illicit drug use was found to exist, to varying degrees, in cities and towns across the UK (except, for particular reasons, in Northern Ireland – see Murray 1994).

The official statistics' limited usefulness, beyond giving very general pointers to trends in drug use, was recognized and attempts were made to create more accurate and useful epidemiological knowledge. One such was the Drug Indicators Project, within Bloomsbury Health Authority, funded by the Department of Health and Social Security (Hartnoll 1985; Hartnoll *et al.* 1985). The project's aim was to generate techniques for estimating prevalence that would be useful in assessing the extent of drug use, and the adequacy of existing services. A variety of methods was employed, which made use of existing data from different sources. The project suggested that Home Office notifications under-represented the number of regular opiate users by at least a factor of five, and possibly one of ten. This gave a figure of around 40,000 people who had used opiates regularly for at least part of the year in 1982 and, the authors argued, a figure nearer 50,000 for 1983. This multiplier became one of the assumptions built into discussions of drug use in the 1980s. The DHSS circulated a manual on how to estimate prevalence, based on the project's work, to health authorities (DHSS 1984), and frequently referred to the five-ten multiplier.

The numbers, even just those thrown up by the Index, but especially those generated by using the Drug Indicators Project multiplier, showed that existing services were inadequate. Turner (1994) identifies the total treatment and rehabilitation services available at the time as 45 NHS Drug Dependency Clinics, most with access to some inpatient beds, and about the same number of voluntary agencies providing day services and residential rehabilitation.

However, from about 1984, the Thatcher government began to develop an interest and a perspective on drug use as an issue and in 1985 the first national strategy, *Tackling Drug Misuse* (Home Office 1985) was published. The five elements described in this document were:

- reducing supplies from abroad;
- making enforcement even more effective;
- strengthening deterrence and tightening domestic controls;
- developing prevention;
- improving treatment and rehabilitation.

The first three of these demonstrate a concern with the supply side of drug use, while the last two are about demand. The whole strategy was overseen by a Ministerial Group on the Misuse of Drugs, set up in July 1984. This included the ministers responsible for drug matters at the Home Office and at the DHSS, and ministers from the Department of Education and Science, the Foreign and Commonwealth Office, Welsh Office, Scottish Office and the Treasury.

However, the most important parts of the strategy, in terms of the concerns of this chapter, were those that were defined as *treatment and rehabilitation* measures. The interest and intervention in drugs policy by central government was new, and this was particularly true of the DHSS. The DHSS in the early 1980s accepted a definition of drug use as an issue in which intervention was needed, adopted a view on what an appropriate model of services was, created a structure within the statutory authorities and particularly the NHS to enact that model, and provided unprecedented amounts of money to fund services. In this sense, it could be said that the Department had a 'drugs policy' for the first time.

The problem drug-taker

A key document was the report of the Advisory Council for the Misuse of Drugs' (ACMD) working group on *Treatment and Rehabilitation* (ACMD 1982), published in December 1982. This set out clearly a particular construction of drug use and the drug user and the task of services, and described a model of service development and a structure for achieving that development. The report was largely adopted by central government and its publication was accompanied by the announcement of a £2 million initiative for services. An account of the main elements of the report was published by the Institute for the Study of Drug Dependence early in 1983 (ISDD 1983), and four commentaries on the report were published in the *British Journal of Addiction* (Ghodse 1983; Slater 1983; Stimson 1983; Yates 1983), making the key ideas of the report accessible widely in the field.

The report introduced the term 'problem drug-taker', one quite consciously borrowed from contemporary thinking in the alcohol field: 'Thus a problem drugtaker would be any person who experiences social, psychological, physical or legal problems related to intoxication and/or regular excessive consumption and/or dependence as a consequence of his own use of drugs or other chemical substances (excluding alcohol and tobacco)' (ACMD 1982: para. 5.13). The significance of this is to redefine drug use away from the narrow conception of addiction. It opens up the range of aspects of a drug user's life of legitimate concern to services. The report pointed away from conceptualizing drug problems as 'short-term diseases', which contact with services could 'cure'. Instead, it conceptualized them in terms of 'chronic handicaps and disorders of behaviour' (para. 5.19). This was a significant shift in the language used in drugs policy, away from the 'addict' and 'addiction'. In practice the terms 'drug misuser' and 'drug misuse' have become the generally accepted ones in policy but these reflect the definition of the problem drug-taker given in the 1982 report (Audit Commission 2002; NTA 2002). The implications of this in service delivery terms was the need for a structure of multi-disciplinary teams, crossing the medical/psychological/social divides, and the involvement of

GPs and other medical non-specialists in what one of the Department's senior medical officers described as 'a flexible locally based network of services able to respond to the wide range of drug related problems' (Black 1988: 84).

This structure had two elements: agencies providing direct services, and advisory and coordinating bodies. The structure was based on the newly-created NHS structure of regional and district health authorities, with the regions given responsibility for implementation, within national guidelines. Regions and districts were first asked to establish a figure for local prevalence of drug use, and were provided with suggestions based on the Drug Indicators Project to do so. They were also required to carry out an audit of existing provision, and to make plans for the development of services within a regional strategy for tackling drug misuse (DHSS 1984, 1985).

Ultimately, multi-disciplinary drug problem teams were expected to be set up at both regional level and district level. These teams were to be direct service providers, but were also to have the important task of involving other professionals, particularly GPs, in the care of drug users, what one consultant involved in setting up such teams called 'turning the generalist on to drugs' (Strang 1989: 143). At both levels, Drug Advisory Committees (RDACs and DDACs) were to be set up, comprising representatives of health, local authority social services and education departments, police, probation and relevant voluntary sector groups.

To fund the development of services, the DHSS provided pump priming money, in the form of the Central Funding Initiative (CFI). The amounts available through the CFI grew from the £2 million announced in December 1982, to a total of £17.5 million in the six years from 1983 to 1989. This money provided a total of 188 grants and was significant in 'adding a layer of community services to the previously existing hospital and residential provision' (MacGregor *et al.* 1991: 6). The CFI was followed by annual allocations of 'specific grants' to health authorities to develop drug services. As MacGregor *et al.* (1991) and Stimson and Lart (1994) have described, the overall social policy framework was one of earmarked allocations from the centre, which protected the status of drugs services as a *national* priority from *local* political decisions. However, against this central direction, there was a relative lack of detail about how services should operate within the broad parameters set by the DHSS' request for strategies. This framework 'allowed for strong central direction accompanied by local autonomy' (Stimson and Lart 1994: 339).

The development of these services proved to be crucial in the response to HIV. In late 1985 the first published findings on HIV seropositivity among injecting drug users in the UK appeared and the possibility for rapid spread became obvious. Testing for seropositivity among groups of injecting drug users in Edinburgh revealed alarmingly high rates of infection: 38 per cent (Peutherer *et al.* 1985) and 51 per cent (Robertson *et al.* 1986a), at a time when the overall rate for England was believed to be around 5 per cent (Robertson *et al.* 1986b). The implications for drug users were compounded by the discovery that blood donated within the Lothian Health Board Region was infected, the first instance of HIV infection in the domestically produced blood supply. The issue rapidly became an urgent one, with concern for drug users themselves matched by the idea that they could be a route for transmission of the virus into the general population.

The provision of clean injecting equipment was first raised by the McClelland Report (SHHD 1986), which looked into the issue of contaminated blood supplies. In the autumn of 1986, and after a visit to Amsterdam to see needle and syringe exchanges operating there (part of an earlier drive to contain Hepatitis B), the then Secretary of State for Health, Norman Fowler, announced that pilot needle and syringe exchanges would be set up in the UK and evaluated for their effectiveness in persuading injectors to reduce sharing equipment. In fact some services had already started to provide clean equipment, something Fowler acknowledged in announcing the pilots (Hansard 1986, col. 703).

Fifteen pilot schemes were set up across England and Scotland in 1987. These were mostly, though not exclusively, in the sorts of community-based services that had developed over the previous few years. Unusually for the time, the evaluation of the schemes was built in from the beginning (Stimson *et al.* 1988; Donoghoe *et al.* 1992; Stimson 2000), an apparently excellent example of rational policy-making. However, the philosophy behind needle exchange was one which resonated so well with the ideas of addressing harm, rather then just drug use itself, and fitted with the broader conceptualization of what services should be doing that had developed in the early 1980s (Stimson and Lart 1991), that developments somewhat pre-empted the outcome of the evaluation and by the time the research group reported there were many more needle exchange schemes operating (Lart and Stimson 1990).

The ACMD had set up a working group on AIDS in May 1987. This group was taking evidence and deliberating during the pilot year, and the first part of its report was published at the end of March 1988, just as the pilot year ended (ACMD 1988). The most often quoted of the report's conclusions was that which echoed the earlier McClelland Report, that 'the spread of HIV is a greater danger to individual and public health than drug misuse' (ACMD 1988: 75).

Needle exchange and other harm minimization practices have gone on to become so much part of normal practice for drugs agencies that it is possible to forget how comparatively recent and potentially radical they were. However, as I have shown, it is possible to see how and why they were so readily adopted in the UK context. Stimson credits the developments of the 1980s with the successful control of the spread of HIV among injecting drug users in the UK (1995), but points out how easily this could be lost by the change in emphasis in policy that followed the election of the Labour government in 1997 (2000).

Current policy

In 1995, the Conservative government had published a three-year drugs strategy in the White Paper *Tackling Drugs Together* (Cm. 2846). This identified three areas for work, communities, young people and public health, and set out the following aims:

- increase the safety of communities from drug-related harm;
- reduce acceptability and availability of drugs to young people;
- reduce the health risks and other damage related to drug misuse.

The new Labour government published its own White Paper, *Tackling Drugs Together to Build a Better Britain* (Cm. 3945) in 1998, which became the ten-year National Strategy. When first published, the Strategy contained four aims:

- to help young people resist drug misuse in order to achieve their full potential in society;
- to protect our communities from drug-related anti-social and criminal behaviour;
- to enable people with drug problems to overcome them and live healthy and crime-free lives;
- to stifle the availability of illegal drugs on our streets.

The 1998 Strategy had dropped the explicit mention of public health and health risks that had been found in the 1995 document. This move away from the centrality of health issues within drugs policy by the new Labour government was noted by commentators such as Stimson (2000), Buchanan and Lee (2000) and Hunt and Stevens (2004). In particular, in a speech to the Methadone Alliance, Gerry Stimson (2000) attacked Labour for launching an 'unhealthy' drug policy, arguing that health issues had been pushed off the policy agenda by an obsession with the conflation of drugs and crime, and the presentation of drugs as a threat to those key New Labour concepts of the family and the community. The achievement of the prevention of widespread transmission of HIV among drug injectors in Britain, by means of harm reduction measures or what Stimson called a 'healthy policy' between 1987 and 1997, had become taken for granted, while the rising rates of other blood-borne diseases, notably hepatitis C, had been ignored. Further, not only was 'health' absent from the policy as a positive goal, but the effects of the policy would be to exacerbate the most 'unhealthy' aspects of drug use – pushing people into the criminal justice system, damaging the relationship that exists in voluntary treatment between user and provider and creating a climate of opinion that stigmatizes and marginalizes the most damaged and needy drug user, a point also made by Buchanan and Lee (2000).

Hunt and Stevens (2004) develop this further, arguing that what has happened in British policy has been a change in the conceptualization of harm. Whereas harm reduction in the 1980s and early 1990s meant reduction of harm *to* the drug user, by the late 1990s it had come to mean harm *by* the drug user, *to* those emblematic families and communities. The underlying assumption to this is that the indisputably large amount of crime that is committed by people who misuse drugs is a *result* of their drug misuse. This assumption has been challenged on the basis that the causal relations are not that clear (Seddon 2000; Stevens *et al.* 2003; Hughes and Anthony, this volume). The outcome of this assumption has been the increased significance of joint work between statutory and independent sector drug treatment services on the one hand, and the criminal justice agencies on the other. In relation to individual drug users, this has meant the development of Drug Treatment and Testing Orders and other forms of 'quasi-compulsory treatment' (Stevens *et al.* 2003), discussed by Hughes and Anthony in their chapter in this volume. Certainly the wording of the 1998 strategy, with the aim of treatment being defined as helping people 'to lead healthy and *crime-free* lives' (my italics) seems to support these analyses. Hunt and Stevens make the point that such coercion is alien to British treatment services which have always operated on a voluntary basis, and that it may have adverse consequences for the nature and quality of services (2003). There are also equity issues: if access to services is prioritized for those who appear in the criminal justice system, the 'criminal needy' (Stimson 2000: 263), where does that leave the non-offending drug misuser who wants help?

Stimson's speech and the concern within the drugs field about the implications of the 1998 Strategy led to the creation of the UK Harm Reduction Alliance, a campaigning body of drugs workers, researchers and users with the aim of ensuring that public health and harm reduction initiatives were strengthened and put back into the national strategies (www.ukhra.org). *The Updated Drug Strategy* (Drugs Strategy Directorate 2002) does include references to harm reduction. The treatment section has been renamed 'Treatment and harm minimisation' (p. 50), and health-related harm reduction measures are discussed. However, the emphasis on crime, and on using the criminal justice system as a means of accessing and channelling drug misusers into treatment is still there, and the majority of new funding has been targeted on criminal justice measures (Audit Commission 2002: 60).

The coordinating structures set up in the 1980s have been developed. In particular, the purchaser/provider split introduced into health and social care services in the early 1990s has been reflected in the strengthened role of the strategic, commissioning bodies.

Drug Action Teams

The 1995 White Paper had set up Drug Action Teams (DATs) in each health authority, building on the District Drug Advisory Committees set up during the 1980s to coordinate local responses. The DATs' role was a strategic one: to assess the nature and scale of local drug problems, ensure that local agencies' work was coordinated and to implement the White Paper locally. Their membership included senior representation from health, police, probation, social services and other local authority departments – education and housing, for example – as well as the prison service and customs and excise (for an early evaluation of the development of the DATs, see Duke and MacGregor 1997).

Changes in structures within the NHS from the late 1990s necessitated changes in responsibility for planning and commissioning drug services. Each DAT is now co-terminous with a local authority – either a shire county, unitary, metropolitan district or London borough. In some (but not all) areas, the DAT has now been combined with the local Crime and Disorder Partnership.

The move to a primary-care led NHS, with the creation of Primary Care Trusts (PCTs) and the abolition of the health authorities in 2002, has moved responsibility within health for commissioning drugs services to the PCTs. Commissioning of drugs services at DAT level is done by joint commissioning groups (JCGs) of the agencies involved in the DAT, or by one of the commissioning authorities (the PCT or local authority for example) either from their own budget, or through pooled funds, or as the lead for funds held by the other authorities. The NHS Act 1999 made possible the creation of such shared budgets. The Audit Commission has identified difficulties in funding arrangements resulting from the potentially different priorities of commissioning agencies and the lack of expertise in commissioning drugs services in agencies because spending on drugs constitutes a small part of the total budget of an agency (something that is likely to be exacerbated with the move from health authorities to smaller PCTs) (Audit Commission 2002: 59–60).

The National Treatment Agency

The National Treatment Agency for Substance Misuse (NTA) was set up as a special health authority in 2001, with the objective of improving effectiveness, efficiency and access to treatment services in England. It does this by providing guidance and support to DATs and others in commissioning services. In particular, the NTA has published a document, *Models of Care* (NTA 2002), discussed below, which has the status of a National Service Framework for adult drug misuse services (another document for services for young drug misusers is currently being prepared).

Effectiveness

A significant strand of current health policy is the development of evidence-based practice and the importance of only funding effective treatment. A review of evidence of the effectiveness of treatment for drug misuse published in 1996 (TaskForce to Review Services for Drug Misusers 1996) demonstrated the lack of good evidence underpinning the treatment given to drug misusers. The idea of evidence-based medicine, or evidence-based practice, has developed as a response to the criticism of Cochrane (1972) that most treatments and procedures available in the NHS had never been systematically evaluated, and the choice in any individual case was the result of historical and local opinion within the medical profession. This, Cochrane argued, raised issues of both effectiveness and equity. Money spent on ineffective treatments was not only useless, but was inequitable as, within limited resources, it meant people were being denied access to effective treatment. Within the drugs field, much of what happened within services, whether in the medically dominated clinics or in multi-agency teams, street agencies or residential rehabilitation services had never been rigorously evaluated and reflected operating philosophies and professional values rather than the application of research findings.

The lack of good data, and particularly the almost complete absence of studies in a UK context, led the Task Force to commission a study of treatment services, the National Treatment Outcomes Research Study (NTORS) (Polkinghorne et al. 2005). This was a multi-site, prospective study of over 1000 drug misusers who entered drug misuse treatment services (residential and community-based) in England in 1995. This study has been central to policy decisions about treatment policies over the last decade. NTORS demonstrated that at one year after intake all the forms of treatment included had positive effects on a whole range of outcome measures, including illicit drug use, social functioning and involvement in crime. This improvement remained for most outcomes at four- or five-year follow up; those not showing sustained improvements were the effects on serious alcohol use and crack/cocaine use (Gossop et al. 1998, 2003). Estimates of the cost benefits of treatment in the study suggested that for every pound spent in treatment, three were saved elsewhere in public spending, notably in the criminal justice and health systems. The results of NTORS have led to the definitive statement that 'treatment works' as the opening statement of the chapter on treatment in the *Updated Drugs Strategy* (Drugs Strategy Directorate 2002: 50).

Other measures to improve and develop standards within the field are the QuADS manual which sets out measurable standards describing minimum and good practice levels of drug and alcohol service provision, developed by Drugscope, and work to create national training and qualification frameworks (Alcohol Concern/SCODA 1999).

Just as the NTA was created, the Audit Commission undertook a review of services for drug misusers (Audit Commission 2002). The review found wide variations and inconsistencies in service delivery, with differing philosophies and practices which were often not evidence-based. This was reinforced by a lack of appropriately skilled staff – while many people in the field were highly qualified, they often did not have specific training for the roles they were carrying out. As a consequence, there were not good quality screening and assessment procedures in place which would effectively match drug misusers presenting to services with the right package of provision for them individually. From the drug misuser's perspective, access was often an issue, with waiting times and inflexible provision in some areas acting as a deterrent to potential users.

At DAT level there was a lack of good, specialist commissioning skills – for most of the agencies involved drugs services were only a small part of their total expenditure, and not a priority. In particular, most attention was given to initiatives and relatively small amounts of new money, rather than wholesale review of mainstream services. DATs needed quick and easy ways of assessing patterns and developments of local need, and better information about existing services in order to be able to carry out such reviews.

At national level, the Commission saw a need for the NTA to take a role in the dissemination of research and the fostering of a research-aware culture, and the building of capacity within the field. Funding on an annual basis was unhelpful and the government should look at ways of developing longer-term and more flexible funding arrangements. Other changes, like alterations in funding for GPs and the development of personal medical services, also open up possibilities while complicating the scene.

The review was carried out just before the *Updated Drugs Strategy* and *Models of Care* were published, but the Commission points to a period of ambitious and rapid change within the field, which would need strategic coordination.

Models of Care – the future for drug services?

The framework presented by *Models of Care* identifies four tiers of services (NTA 2002: 20):

- *Tier 1, non-substance misuse-specific services requiring interface with drug and alcohol treatment*, e.g. primary care for general health problems, supported housing.
- *Tier 2, open access drug misuse services*, e.g. advice and information, needle exchange, drop in, outreach service, low-threshold prescribing, assessment.
- *Tier 3, structured community-based specialist drug misuse services*, e.g.

structured treatment plan, structured counselling, prescribing, treatment element of Drug Treatment and Testing Orders.

- *Tier 4a, residential substance misuse services*, e.g. inpatient detoxification services, residential rehabilitation services.
- *Tier 4b, highly specialized non-substance misuse-specific specific services*, e.g. young people's hospital and residential services, HIV specialist units, liver disease units.

The document also introduces the idea of integrated care pathways: protocols to standardize routes into and out of treatment, and the aims, objectives and process of treatment. The aim is to ensure there is effective coordination and communication between the different services meeting a given individual's needs, and to ensure consistency and equity nationally.

A major influence within the drugs field in recent years has been the 'Trans-theoretical Model' or 'Stages of Change' (Prochaska and DiClemente 1983). This model argues that behaviour change involves a series of stages that an individual goes through, prior to change. These are: pre-contemplation, contemplation, preparation, action and maintenance. A possible further stage is that of relapse, which can take the individual back to any of the previous stages in the process. The tiers of services outlined in *Models of Care* can be mapped onto this model with Tiers 1 and 2 supporting, and keeping healthy, people still in pre-contemplation or contemplation phases. The model has also drawn attention to the need for services to prevent or respond to relapse. Similarly, *Models of Care* draws up a hierarchy of aims for the provision of drug services which also recognizes the significance of steps short of reducing or stopping drug use, and does seem to address the criticisms made of policy in the wake of the 1998 White Paper (NTA 2002: 11).

In many ways, *Models of Care* represents a new departure: as well as clarifying responsibilities for planning and commissioning, it is an attempt to create a national standard for the organization and delivery of services. In comparison with the centrally-driven but locally autonomous nature of developments in the 1980s, described earlier, the current policy framework reflects the increasing centralization of the detail of delivery that has been a feature of recent health policy.

Conclusions

A key theme of current drugs policy is coordination. This is not new – from the early 1980s there have been successive attempts to improve joint working between services at the operational level as well as at the planning and commissioning level. Many of the issues that arise are not unique to the drugs field; issues of conflicting professional agendas and philosophies, mismatched organizational structures and differing priorities have dogged inter-agency working in social policy for decades (Cameron and Lart 2003). The shape of drug services has in the past been very dependent on the historical developments of a given locality. This in turn has depended on the interests and philosophies of key players locally – consultant psychiatrists who had an interest in drug misuse, the strength and focus of local voluntary sector organizations, the degree to which agencies like health, social services and probation have worked together in a given area. However, the moves by the DHSS in the early 1980s were an early version of what is being attempted through the NTA and *Models of Care*. In the 1980s, a model of service development was offered, and funds made available through the Central Funding Initiative and subsequently through annual specific grants to health authorities, for the development of services in line with that model. The difference now may prove to be the extent to which centrally the Department of Health, through the NTA, can drive the shape and detail of provision at a local level. Changing financial possibilities, through pooled budgets and other mechanisms, start to open up the possibilities for genuinely shared working. Central to this will be the development of commissioning skills at DAT level and the support that the NTA can give.

A further theme is that of ensuring the provision of effective and high-quality services. The historical development of drugs services has led to the wide variations in practice and styles identified by the Audit Commission. The specific framing of this is new and reflects the development of the philosophy of evidence-based practice. The lack of an evidence base has started to be addressed by the results of NTORS, which gave a welcome endorsement to the provision of treatment in its widest sense. However, much more detailed knowledge of which individuals benefit most from which types of treatment services is needed to underpin the development of detailed assessment and the ability to tailor packages of care for individuals.

The critique of Stimson and others that policy has become led too much by a concern with crime still holds, despite the return of specific health aims and targets in *The Updated Drugs Strategy*. Most of the new money for treatment will be used in the provision of the treatment elements of Drug Treatment and Testing Orders or their successors. I started this chapter by saying drugs were a 'wicked issue'; one which crosses sectoral boundaries, and for which there are no universally agreed definitions and desired outcomes. It is in the relationship between health-related services and the criminal justice system that this becomes clearest. For a long time the two operated separate agendas around drugs, even while the reality of drug users' lives reflected their interconnectedness, and better coordination should be applauded. However, the current close relationship represents more than just a concern for coordination. It reflects a particular view of *why* drug users should be encouraged to undertake treatment: to reduce the harm they are perceived to do to communities and families through their presumed criminal activities. At the start of this chapter, the way that health/medical policy responses to drug users always have to be understood within the broader criminal justice framework was signalled. Despite the amendments contained in *The Updated Drugs Strategy*, and the focus on ensuring high-quality, effective and evidence-based services, it seems clear that the current policy phase has to be seen as one in which the health and welfare approach to drug users is subsumed into the concerns of criminal justice policy.

References

ACMD (1982) *Treatment and Rehabilitation: Report of the Advisory Council on the Misuse of Drugs*. London: HMSO.

ACMD (1988) *AIDS and Drug Misuse Part 1: Report by the Advisory Council on the Misuse of Drugs*. London: HMSO.

Alcohol Concern/SCODA (1999) *QuADS: Organisational Standards for Alcohol and Drug Treatment Services*. London: Alcohol Concern/SCODA.

Audit Commission (2002) *Changing Habits: The Commissioning and Management of Community Drug Treatment Services for Adults*. London: Audit Commission.

Berridge, V. (1980) The making of the Rolleston Report 1908–1926, *Journal of Drug Issues*, Winter.

Berridge, V. (1984) Drugs and social policy: the establishment of drug control in Britain 1900–1930, *British Journal of Addiction*, 79: 17–29.

Berridge, V. and Edwards, G. (1987) *Opium and the People: Opiate use in Nineteenth Century England*. London: Yale University Press.

Berridge, V. and Edwards, G. (1998) *Opium and the People: Opiate Use and Policy in 19th and Early 20th Century Britain*. London: Free Association Books.

Bevan, A. (1952) *In place of fear*. London: Heinemann.

BJA (1988) Conversation with H.B. Spear, *British Journal of Addiction*, 83: 473–82.

Black, D. (1988) Drug misuse: policy and service development, *Journal of the Royal Society of Health*, 3: 83–9.

Buchanan, J. and Lee, Y. (2000) The war on drugs – a war on drug users? *Drugs: Education, Prevention and Policy*, 7: 409–22.

Cameron, A. and Lart, R. (2003) Factors promoting and obstacles hindering joint working, *Journal of Integrated Care*, 11: 9–17.

Cm. 2846 (1995) *Tackling Drugs Together*. London: The Stationary Office.

Cm. 3945 (1998) *Tackling Drugs Together to Build a Better Britain*, London: The Stationary Office.

Cochrane, A. (1972) *Effectiveness and Efficiency: Random Reflections on Health Services*. Oxford: Nuffield Provincial Hospital Trust.

Connell, P. and Strang, J. (1994) The creation of the clinics: clinical demand and the formation of policy, in J. Strang and M. Gossop (eds) *Heroin Addiction and Drug Policy: The British System*. Oxford: Oxford University Press.

Connell, P. and Strang, J. (2005) The origins of the new drug clinics of the 1960s: clinical demand and the formation of policy, in J. Strang and M. Gossop (eds) *Heroin Addiction and the British System*, vol. II. London: Routledge.

Davenport-Hines, R. (2002) *The Pursuit of Oblivion: A Social History of Drugs*, London: Phoenix Press.

DHSS (1984) *Health Services Development: Services for Drug Misusers, HC(84)14*. London: DHSS.

DHSS (1985) *Drug Misuse: Prevalence and Service Provision: A Report on Surveys and Plans in English National Health Service Regions*. London: DHSS.

Donoghoe, M.C., Stimson, G.V. and Dolan, K.A. (1992) *Syringe Exchanges in England: An Overview*. London: The Tufnell Press.

Dorn, N. and South, N. (1994) The power behind practice drug control and harm minimization in inter-agency and criminal law contexts, in J. Strang and M. Gossop (eds) *Heroin Addiction and Drug Policy: The British System*. Oxford: Oxford University Press.

Drugs Strategy Directorate (2002) *The Updated Drugs Strategy*. London: Home Office.

Duke, K. and MacGregor, S. (1997) *Tackling Drugs Locally: The Implementation of Drug Action Teams in England*. London: HMSO.

Fazey, C. (1979) In the heroin trap, *Guardian*, 30 October.

Ghodse, H. (1983) View from a clinic: need for action on a revised response, *British Journal of Addiction*, 78: 115–18.

Glanz, A. and Taylor, C. (1986) Findings of a national survey of the role of general practitioners in the treatment of opiate misuse; extent of contact, *British Medical Journal*, 293: 427–30.

Gossop, M., Marsden, J. and Stewart, D. (1998) *NTORS at one year: the National Treatment Outcome Research Study. Changes in Substance Use, Health and Criminal Behaviours at 1 Year after Intake*. London: Department of Health.

Gossop, M., Marsden, J., Stewart, D. and Kidd, T. (2003) The National Treatment Outcome Research Study (NTORS): 4–5 year follow-up results, *Addiction*, 98: 291–303.

Hansard (1986) *House of Commons Written Answers, 18 December*. London: HMSO.

Harding, G. (1988) *Opiate Addiction, Morality and Medicine: From Moral Illness to Pathological Disease*. London: Macmillan.

Harding, G. (1998) Pathologising the soul: the construction of a 19th century analysis of opiate addiction, in R. Coomber (ed.) *The Control of Drugs and Drug Users: Reason or Reaction?* The Netherlands: Harwood Academic Publishers.

Hartnoll, R. (1985) *The Nature and Extent of Drug Problems in London*. London: Drug Indicators Project, Birkbeck College.

Hartnoll, R., Mitcheson, M., Lewis, R. and Bryer, S. (1985) Estimating the prevalence of opioid dependence, *The Lancet*, i: 203–5.

Holloway, S.W.F. (1995) The regulation of the supply of drugs in Britain before 1868, in R. Porter and M. Teich (eds) *Drugs and Narcotics in History*. Cambridge: Cambridge University Press.

Home Office (1985) *Tackling Drug Misuse: A Summary of the Government's Strategy*, Ist edn. London: HMSO.

Hunt, N. and Stevens, A. (2004) Whose harm? Harm reduction and the shift to coercion in UK drug policy, *Social Policy and Society*, 3: 333–42.

Interdepartmental Committee on Drug Addiction (1965) *Report*. London: HMSO.

ISDD (1983) Advisory Council reports on treatment and rehabilitation, *Druglink Information Letter*, 18: 1–5.

Jay, M. (2000) *Emperors of Dreams: Drugs in the Nineteenth Century*. Cambridge: Dedalus.

Klein, R. (1995) *The New Politics of the NHS*, 2nd edn. Harlow: Longman.

Lart, R. (1998) Medical power/knowledge: the treatment and control of drugs and drug users, in R. Coomber (ed.) *The Control of Drugs and Drug Users: Reason or Reaction?* The Netherlands: Harwood Academic Publishers.

Lart, R.A. and Stimson, G.V. (1990) National survey of syringe-exchange schemes in England, *British Journal of Addiction*, 85: 1433–43.

Lindesmith, A. (1972) The British system of narcotics control, in J. Susman (ed.) *Drug Use and Social Policy*. New York: AMS Press.

MacGregor, S., Ettorre, B., Coomber, R., Crosier, A. and Lodge, H. (1991) *Drugs Services in England and the Impact of the Central Funding Initiative*, ISDD Research Monograph One. London: Institute for the Study of Drug Dependence.

Mitcheson, M. (1994) Drug clinics in the 1970s, in J. Strang and M. Gossop (eds) *Heroin Addiction and Drug Policy: The British System*. Oxford: Oxford University Press.

Mott, J. (1994) Notification and the Home Office, in J. Strang and M. Gossop (eds) *Heroin Addiction and Drug Policy: The British System*. Oxford: Oxford University Press.

Mott, J. and Bean, P. (1998) The development of drug control in Britain, in R. Coomber (ed.) *The Control of Drugs and Drug Users: Reason or Reaction?* The Netherlands: Harwood Academic Publishers.

Murray, M. (1994) Use of illegal drugs in Northern Ireland, in J. Strang and M. Gossop (eds) *Heroin Addiction and Drug Policy: The British System*. Oxford: Oxford University Press.

NTA (2002) *Models of Care for Treatment of Adult Drug Misusers*. London: National Treatment Agency.

O'Hare, P.A., Newcombe, R., Matthews, A., Buning, E. and Drucker, E. (1992) *The Reduction of Drug Related Harm*. London: Routledge.

Pearson, G. (1987) *The New Heroin Users*. London: Blackwell.

Peutherer, J.F., Edmond, E. and Simonds, P. (1985) HTLV-lll antibody in Edinburgh drug addicts, *The Lancet*, 2: 1129–30.

Polkinghorne, J., Gossop, M. and Strang, J. (2005) The Government Task Force and its review of drug treatment services: the promotion of an evidence based approach, in J. Strang and M. Gossop (eds) *Heroin Addiction and the British System, Volume II: Treatment and Policy Responses*. London: Routledge.

Prochaska, J.O. and DiClemente, C.C. (1983) Stages and processes of self-change of smoking: toward an integrative model of change, *Journal of Consulting and Clinical Psychology*, 51: 390–5.

Rittel, H. and Webber, M. (1973) Dilemmas in a general theory of planning, *Policy Sciences*, 4: 155–69.

Robertson, R., Bucknall, A.B.V. and Welsby, P.D. (1986a) Epidemic of AIDS related virus (HTLV-lll/LAV) infection among intravenous drug users, *British Medical Journal*, 292: 527–30.

Robertson, R., Bucknall, A.B.V. and Wiggens, P. (1986b) Regional variations in HIV antibody seropositivity in British intravenous drug users, *The Lancet*, 1435–6.

Schur, E. (1961) British Narcotics Policies, *Journal of Criminal Law and Criminology*, 51, 619–29.

Schur, E. (1963) *Heroin Addiction in Britain and America: the Impact of Public Policy*. London: Tavistock.

Seddon, T. (2000) Explaining the drug-crime link: theoretical, policy and research issues, *Journal of Social Policy*, 29: 95–107.

SHHD (1986) *HIV Infection in Scotland: Report of the Scottish Committee on HIV Infection and Intravenous Drug Misuse*. Edinburgh: SHHD.

Slater, T. (1983) View from a therapeutic community: the spirit of the thing, *British Journal of Addiction*, 78: 118–19.

Smart, C. (1984) Social policy and drug addiction, *British Journal of Addiction*, 79: 31–9.

South, N. (1998) Tackling drug control in Britain: from Sir Malcolm Delevingne to the New Drugs Strategy, in R. Coomber (ed.) *The Control of Drugs and Drug Users: Reason or Reaction?* The Netherlands: Harwood Academic Publishers.

Spear, H.B. (1994) The early years of the 'British System' in practice, in J. Strang and M. Gossop (eds) *Heroin Addiction and Drug Policy: The British System*. Oxford: Oxford University Press.

Stevens, A., Berto, B., Kerschl, V., Oeuvray, K., van Ooyen, M., Steffan, E., Heckmann, W. and Uchtenhagen, A. (2003) *Summary Literature Review: The International Literature on Drugs, Crime and Treatment*. Canterbury: EISS, University of Kent at Canterbury.

Stimson, G.V. (1983) Views of a sociologist: drug problems as an everyday part of our society, *British Journal of Addiction*, 78: 120–2.

Stimson, G.V. (1994) Minimising harm from drug use, in J. Strang and M. Gossop (eds) *Heroin Addiction and Drug Policy: The British System*. Oxford: Oxford University Press.

Stimson, G.V. (1995) AIDS and injecting drug use in the United Kingdom 1987–1993: the policy response and the prevention of the epidemic, *Social Science and Medicine*, 41: 699–716.

Stimson, G.V. (2000) 'Blair declares war': the unhealthy state of British drug policy, *International Journal of Drug Policy*, 11: 259–64.

Stimson, G.V. and Lart, R.A. (1991) HIV, drugs, and public health in England: new words, old tunes, *International Journal of the Addictions*, 26: 1263–77.

Stimson, G.V. and Lart, R.A. (1994) The relationship between the state and local practice in the development of national policy on drugs between 1920 and 1990, in J. Strang and M. Gossop (eds) *Heroin Addiction and Drug Policy: The British System*, vol. II. London: Routledge.

Stimson, G.V., Alldritt, L., Dolan, K., Donoghoe, M.C. and Lart, R.A. (1988) *Injecting Equipment Exchange Schemes: Final Report*. London: Goldsmiths' College.

Strang, J. (1989) A model service: turning the generalist on to drugs, in S. MacGregor, (ed.) *Drugs and British Society: Responses to a Social Problem in the 1980s*. London: Routledge.

Strang, J. and Gossop, M. (1994) The British system: visionary anticipation or masterly inactivity? in J. Strang and M. Gossop (eds) *Heroin Addiction and Drug Policy: The British System*. Oxford: Oxford University Press.

Strang, J. *et al.* (2005) The history of prescribing heroin and other injectable drugs as addiction treatment in the UK, in J. Strang and M. Gossop (eds) *Heroin Addiction and the British System*, vol. II. London: Routledge.

Task Force to Review Services for Drug Misusers (1996) *Report of an Independent Review of Drug Treatment Services in England*. London: DoH.

Trebach, A. (1982) *The Heroin Solution*. New Haven, CT: Yale University Press.

Turner, D. (1994) The development of the voluntary sector: no further need for pioneers? in J. Strang and M. Gossop (eds) *Heroin Addiction and Drug Policy: The British System*. Oxford: Oxford University Press.

Yates, R. (1983) View from a street agency: money-shy, *British Journal of Addiction*, 78: 122–4.

Further reading

Berridge, V. and Edwards, G. (1998) *Opium and the People: Opiate Use and Policy in 19th and Early 20th Century Britain*. London: Free Association Books.

Coomber, R. (ed.) *The Control of Drugs and Drug Users: Reason or Reaction?* The Netherlands: Harwood Academic Publishers.

NTA (2002) *Models of Care for Treatment of Adult Drug Misusers*. London: National Treatment Agency.

Strang, J. and Gossop, M. (eds) (2005) *Heroin Addiction and the British System, Volume II: Treatment and Policy Responses*. London: Routledge.

Drifting Towards a More Common Approach to a More Common Problem: Epidemiology and the Evolution of a European Drug Policy

Henri Bergeron and Paul Griffiths

Introduction

Few policy developments in Europe are easy to describe. Difficulties are magnified when we consider European drug policy, an area which until recently many would claim simply did not exist. And in a strictly formal, legal sense this is true: no EU policy on drugs does exist as there is no legal basis available for policy development in this area.

Furthermore, the odds against the development of European policy in this area appear rather high. The drugs issue cuts across a range of controversial topics ranging from basic rights and freedoms, through public health policies including HIV prevention, to criminal justice responses. There appears to be no clear consensus within member states on many aspects of these issues and this fact cannot facilitate the development of a consensus at the European level. On the official level, policy on illicit drugs remains an area where subsidiarity reigns supreme and no competencies are given to the institutions. Can we in a Europe that encompasses coffee shops in the Netherlands and a Swedish policy of zero tolerance talk meaningfully about a European perspective? And, what evidence is there for a common approach in what appear to be areas of clear policy divergence? Add to this mix the new member states, who until recently had a past experience of illicit drug problems that shared little with those of the former 15 members, and one might be forgiven for thinking that even the notion of a common policy is somewhat absurd. Yet slowly we have seen the gradual evolution of what is now beginning to look like a European policy perspective on drugs. In evolutionary terms what has emerged may be a somewhat strange beast, but nonetheless, commonalities are increasingly apparent in the way European countries address drugs issues. And although no formal EU policy exists, a number of structures and actions at the European level coordinate and facilitate activities, and increasingly we are beginning to hear a stronger European voice in the international debate on drug issues.

It would still be wrong to overemphasize the cohesive nature of European drug policy. In many respects what exists is a developing, practical accomplishment, where the focus is on areas of consensus within a perspective that provides sufficient latitude for national differences. In this it is no different from other controversial policy areas faced by the European project. If our analysis is to be comprehensive, it should be informed by a broader reflection on the development of the Union and on the subsidiarity debate. Here, however, our task is more modest; we seek only to identify some of the evidence that suggests there has been a drift towards a more common approach to European drug policy and to identify some of the factors specific to the drugs issue that have played a part in this process. In a simple analysis we would argue that this process includes: the gradual development, and the political recognition, of a more common experience of the drug phenomenon across Europe; a growing commitment in what is a highly ideological area to try and give the policy debate a scientific and rational foundation; and the accompanying development of methods to collect and analyse data to allow comparison, resulting in the subsequent acceptance of the need for institutional structures to collect and analyse information at the European level.

European drug policies: a drift towards convergence?

To begin to answer the question 'how have European drug policies evolved?' one must first go back and consider the situation 20 or so years ago. This is not in itself a simple task, as detailed information sources remain limited and it is easy to forget how profoundly different the political, social and economic landscape then looked. What can be said with confidence is that European drugs policies were fundamentally different from each other at that time and if they could be characterized by anything it was their diversity. With respect to how the drugs issue was perceived, what policies existed? Here there were considerable differences between national policies across Europe; they were both punitive and socially orientated. Treatment services, where they existed, differed, legal responses differed, and in some countries drug problems had still to arrive as an issue of national concern. As we put it elsewhere in a more detailed discussion (Bergeron 2005a, 2005b), public policies in this domain were defined at that time on the basis of a rationale that was essentially national, marked by the social, institutional and cultural characteristics of each of the member states. If we contrast this situation with the picture today, in simple terms at least it has not changed radically: European drug policies remain different, particularly with regard to availability and to the level of implementation of interventions. Any conscientious observer knows that European drug policies are often portrayed, in particular in political discourse, as being inspired by and framed in different and incompatible values. This political reality is hard to deny, yet evidence is also available that supports the assumption of a relative convergence of European drug policies. One must be clear here that 'convergence' does not mean that drug policies have become identical. Rather, the distinction made when translating languages should apply between identity and equivalence. A word in one language is not strictly identical to that in another, but it has an *equivalent*. This perhaps applies to national drug policies in Europe in that they are far from identical but follow equivalent paths.

We will consider, for the purpose of illustration, four examples of this growth in policy equivalence. The first of these is perhaps the least well documented. It is the notion of an overarching drug policy itself or, more precisely, the framing of policy initiatives within the context of an overall strategy and action plan. The spread in adoption of this approach means that strategies and action plans are adopted that define precise priorities and objectives, that implicitly or explicitly require routine monitoring of activities, that foresee time-bound achievements, and that envisage ad hoc evaluation schemes and processes. This is a new phenomenon for Europe as a whole but is now widespread and means that drug policies have the formal appearance of policies in other areas. And as with other policy areas, there is an increasingly increasing tendency to adapt tools and concepts originally developed for managing private companies into the culture of public sector evaluation and planning. From this perspective, a modern drug policy should include an initial assessment of the epidemiological situation and should set up an information system allowing both the routine monitoring of the strategy's achievements and an assessment of its effectiveness. Ideally, interventions of every type should be evaluated to justify their legitimacy and also perhaps their cost-effectiveness, even if this means that the concept of evaluation is sometimes stretched to, and sometimes beyond, its methodological breaking point. This remains a key ingredient, necessary for programme development. There must be an 'evidence base' for guiding action, a term now so widely used that it has become almost the ubiquitous mantra of every conference and policy-making forum.

All this may appear an obvious observation today but it is easy to forget that this was not the fashion of the past. In Europe as a whole, it was not so long ago that the idea of evaluating drug treatment programmes, according to methodological protocols used in other sectors of medicine would have been considered by many to be, if not absurd, at least an unproductive approach. We are not proposing here that there has been a simple adoption of a positivist approach where science alone guides policy. Clearly this is not the case, since the findings of research and evaluation are rarely exhaustive, and neither do they remove all ambiguities and, therefore, include a large measure of uncertainty. As other commentators have noted, the relationship between research and policy in the drugs field is a complex one and not reducible to a simple cause and effect model (Berridge and Stanton 1999). Frequently, research findings open the door rationally to several possible scenarios and policy-makers can be selective in identifying the evidence that fits best with policy perspectives already developed. Here, scientific evidence and evaluation research should be regarded as enlightening rather than defining policy, and as such they do not replace or even necessarily shape policy decision-making. However, the contrast that can be made between European policy-making today and the historical situation is that a drug policy cannot ground its legitimacy *solely* on a moral rationale, as was the case to a large extent in the 1970s. There is now a growing pressure for states to be accountable to their citizens for what they do, how they do it and for the results they achieve. The European drug debate may still have its moral and ideological dimensions but they must increasingly coexist with an empirical model that demands that our actions be evidence-based and evaluated.

The second example we offer of convergence is the increasing acceptance of harm-reduction policies and opioid substitution treatment across Europe. It should be noted that the development of both these areas has to be seen in the wider context of European countries' experiences of the HIV epidemic and the resulting need to include HIV prevention measures as an important policy objective. History shows us that in Europe drug-free treatment and abstinence-orientated programmes in many countries were the first kind of treatment to be developed. These treatments have never been particularly controversial, although at times the settings and the conditions under which they were implemented raised debate among experts in certain countries – for example, the discussions about therapeutic communities in France during the 1970s. On the other hand, substitution treatment, other than for short-term withdrawal, has in all countries at times been seen as a more controversial issue, and considerable differences have existed between European countries, and within countries over time, in terms of the availability and type of treatment offered. In particular, access to this kind of treatment has often been highly restrictive.

Although differences in perspective are still evident they are now considerably less marked. Substitution treatment globally has lost for a large part its controversial character and is an integral part of the drug strategies of many member states. Virtually every EU member state has some substitution treatment provision, although activities in this area are generally on a smaller scale in some of the Nordic countries and in some of the new member states. It is worth noting that the growth of substitution treatment represents the major type of increase in the availability of drug treatment in Europe and thus plays a key role in meeting this policy objective. As noted in the annual report of the EMCDDA (2005a), between 1997 and 1998 there was an increase in the overall availability of medically-assisted treatment probably by at least one third. Methadone remains the most widely used pharmacological agent for opioid substitution, although other agents like buprenorphine are now becoming more popular. At least 400,000 people now receive some form of substitution treatment in the 15 'older' member states and Norway, a figure that rises to over half a million if the 10 new member states and the remaining candidate countries are included. It should be remembered that not so long ago opioid substitution therapies, when not used for aiding withdrawal, were considered by many to be a harm reduction measure rather than a part of formal drug treatment. They have now slowly moved to be seen as a mainstay of many countries' treatment sectors, accompanied by a move away from restricting access to encouraging its uptake.

Harm reduction responses themselves remain more controversial, although to some extent the concept of harm reduction as one part of a comprehensive drug strategy has now become widely accepted – even if sometimes to achieve consensus the term itself is not used. Some of the interventions included under the heading of harm reduction – for example, 'consumption rooms' – remain politically sensitive and generate considerable debate on their appropriateness. Other areas, which were once seen as controversial, such as syringe exchanges, low threshold centres, outreach work and so on, no longer attract much critical attention and have become to a large extent recognized as a legitimate part of drug strategy and even as priority areas in some countries. This tendency has been noted at European level, and in June 2003, the Council of Ministers passed a recommendation on 'the prevention and reduction of health-related harm associated with drug dependence'. This text constitutes a major development in the field of public health, since it is the first time that, after having adopted several drug-demand reduction *resolutions*, an EU *recommendation* was adopted. Another significant and recent example is the thematic paper on the role of syringe provision in the reduction of infectious disease incidence and prevalence. This was endorsed by EU member states within the EU Council and drafted by the EMCDDA just before the 2005 CND session, in order to support a mutually agreed position on this kind of intervention. This example demonstrates not only the common recognition of the value of some harm reduction interventions when placed in the overall context of a drug strategy containing a balance of supply and demand side measures, but also the role of scientific evidence in underpinning the adoption of a European common position.

The third example we offer is commonalities in the direction of policies in respect of the legal status granted to the use of drugs, without any aggravating circumstances, or to possession of drugs for personal use. In terms of both European legislation and policies, countries were deeply divided only ten years ago as to what responses were appropriate for discouraging the possession of controlled substances for personal use.

To some extent, at least in the 15 'older' member states, this has changed, especially in regard to, but not restricted to, cannabis. Some countries have amended their laws so that the use of illicit drugs or their possession in small quantities for personal use, while still formally prohibited, is less liable to jail sentences. There has also been a corresponding move to divert drug users from the criminal justice system towards treatment services, although the extent to which this actually occurs varies considerably by drug type and country. Elsewhere, countries have chosen to frame the official response by means of orders or circulars (or other legal instruments) in the same direction (for details of the different legal approaches of countries in Europe to drug possession see EMCDDA 2005b).

Almost everywhere, alternatives to prosecution and to prison, including compulsory treatment, have increased in Europe. This illustrates that the dominant paradigm across member states has shifted to seeing drug problems as requiring social and medical responses rather than punitive ones. Punishment is beginning to be seen as more appropriate for those that profit from drugs or for those whose drug use is aggravated by anti-social behaviour. Thus, irrespective of the legal solution chosen, and apart from the remaining deep differences in national systems, there does seem to be a tendency in the old member states to consider the use of illicit drugs, or possession for personal use, as a more 'minor' offence, in so far as – and only in so far as – jail sentences seem to be avoided and therapeutic measures given preference.

Finally, the fourth of these examples of convergence relates to the progressive but still uneven inclusion of specific mention of licit drugs in the illicit drugs policies of many countries. However, it is not clear to what extent this generic approach is always reflected in terms of implementation. Preliminary work on this topic (Zobel *et al.* 2004) notes that now the majority of European countries do at least mention licit drugs in their illicit drugs strategy and thus the policies are becoming more generic. Of course, there are various levels of integration, ranging from policies that foresee a common approach for prevention work, where models of good practice increasingly suggest a holistic approach, through to policies on substance consumption where illicit drugs are included alongside alcohol and tobacco. Beyond this, some drug strategies also consider 'common provisions' for treatment, harm reduction interventions and for measures aiming at controlling drug markets. Objectives directed at the prevention of all psychoactive substances in the EU are found in the EU action plan (2000 to 2004) (European Commission 1999), and also in either the drug strategy or the action plan of Denmark, Finland, Greece, Ireland, Italy, Luxembourg, the Netherlands, Portugal, England, France and Sweden.

Factors that encourage the drift to convergence

It is perhaps not surprising that drug policies in Europe 20 years ago shared so few commonalities. To a large extent this reflected the different experiences that countries had of the drugs problem. Across Europe as a whole, the prevalence of drug use of all types was lower and largely concentrated in a few countries, mostly in the North of Europe. Even within these countries drug use was often socially, demographically and/or geographically quite closely defined. In the countries of the former Soviet bloc, drug use with a few exceptions was, if not unknown, then certainly unacknowledged and in many countries of southern Europe rates of use were extremely low, to the extent that arguably some of these countries could simply be described as not having a significant drug problem at this time.

Patterns of drug use in European countries still vary considerably, especially in respect of the scale of the problem. That said, and even though prevalence rates still vary, European countries have to a large extent a similar experience of changing patterns of drug use over time. Although the timetable of events may be slightly different, virtually all European countries share some experience of increasing levels of drug use among young people and an epidemic spread of problematic heroin use occurring at some point during the 1980s or 1990s. This spread, the appearance of the AIDS pandemic and the recognition of injecting drug users as a key risk group in Europe also acted to galvanize the attention of practitioners and policy-makers alike. Today it is true that patterns of drug use vary widely in Europe and the difference between high prevalence countries and the lowest prevalence countries remains considerable. Regardless of the measure used, however, more countries now fall in the middle zone of most scales, prevalence rates are generally at historically high levels and new trends in drug use appear to have the ability to quickly transcend national borders. Although it would be wrong to suggest that young people in Europe now share a common cultural identity it would be equally wrong to ignore the fact that aspects of youth culture and experience are now far less geographically delineated than was historically the case. During the early- to mid-1990s the spread across Europe of rave culture and the accompanying use of the drug ecstasy demonstrated how quickly new patterns of drug use could become European in nature. In summary, policy-makers in European countries are not necessarily facing the same scale of problem but they increasingly share a common experience of the drug phenomenon. If we consider policy-makers from Sweden, a country with one of the lowest rates of drug use in Europe, meeting their counterparts from the UK, a country with some of the highest, what is striking is how much they share a common understanding of the issues of importance even if they may sometimes differ on what are the most appropriate responses.

If European policy-makers now share to some extent a common perception of the problem, there has been a corresponding development of information resources to provide what has sometimes been called a common language to support their discourse. At the heart of this approach has been the adoption of a set of common methods and reporting standards to describe in a technically sound and comparable fashion important aspects of the European drug phenomenon. Both authors of the present text are part of the EMCDDA, a decentralized, technical agency of the European Commission, founded in 1993. The rationale behind the EMCDDA was to provide objective and comparable information on the European drug situation. That such a structure and such information is acknowledged as necessary is arguably further evidence of the development of a European drug policy perspective. But it is also evidence of the process touched upon earlier of bringing a scientific and evidence-based approach into the policy arena.

One note of caution: the perspective provided here is limited and narrowly focused on development of modern European policy. As noted by Musto and Sloboda (2003) the use and sometimes misuse of statistics to inform drug policy developments is not new. 'Evidence' on both the nature and the scale of the problem accompanied the prohibition of drug use in the first place. As such, the European story needs to be placed in a broader international perspective and informed by the specific experiences of those member states who have been particularly influential in this area. We have room here only to highlight a few of the important milestones in the development of the European picture (see Hartnoll 2003 for a more detailed review). Among the more important of these is the proposal made by the French president Georges Pompidou in 1971 to strengthen European cooperation and coordination, which would include carrying out joint epidemiological studies. Originally, this programme was simply an inter-governmental communication mechanism, but subsequently in 1980 it was formally attached to the Council of Europe. In December 1982 an expert meeting was held on the development of administrative monitoring systems for the assessment of public health and social problems related to drug use. This in turn led to the formation of an expert epidemiology group that met regularly, together with the launching of, among other projects, a multi-city study that adopted a multi-indicator approach (see Bless 2003). The expert epidemiology group was finally stood down in 2004, when EU enlargement had finally removed the last rationale for its existence and all routine monitoring activities by then had been institutionalized under the responsibility of the EMCDDA. However, the influence of this group cannot be underestimated. Most of what now constitutes the European epidemiological evidence base on drugs, including the key indicators and the European School Survey Project on Alcohol and other Drugs (ESPAD), have their roots in the work of this expert committee.

The role of Europe

The EU does not have many powers and competencies that relate directly to the drugs field. This topic is complex and elaborated in more detail elsewhere (Bergeron 2005a, 2005c). The European 'acquis' on drugs is limited and has not been significantly developed since an explicit reference to illicit drugs was introduced for the first time in the Amsterdam Treaty of 1993. Reference to drugs is also made in a variety of legal documents, scattered throughout the three pillars of the Maastricht Treaty. In a nutshell, the EU does not have global competence in the field of drugs as it does in areas such as agriculture or the environment, in which the EU represents the interests of its member states. The EU can contribute to the effort made by its member states through indirect channels but this is done while fully respecting the treaties and acts and the principle of subsidiarity. To sum up, the EU commitment on drugs is as follows: in the field of drug demand reduction since the Maastricht Treaty, as in the field of public health in general, the EU complements member states' actions in reducing drugs-related health damage, and in providing prevention and information measures. In the field of drug supply reduction, counter-trafficking and drug-related criminality, the Maastricht Treaty provides for police and judicial cooperation in criminal matters and calls for the harmonization of national trafficking laws.

In this context, the adoption of the framework decision on drugs trafficking in 2004 was a major step, laying down minimum provisions on the constituent elements of criminal acts and penalties in the field of drug trafficking. The EU also currently places particular emphasis on dealing with new synthetic drugs and their chemical precursors, as well as combating money-laundering. In the area of international cooperation and external relations, and in all the areas described above, since drugs are a global phenomenon, the EU takes international action with a combination of political initiatives, like the action plans and the dialogue on drugs with various regions of the world, as well as assisting through development programmes. There are other domains in which there is an EU investment; for example, for chemical precursors, which can be diverted into the manufacturing of illicit drugs. EU legislation provides a framework for control of trade in precursors both within the Union and with other countries. But there is, as mentioned above, no formal EU policy on drugs and member states have kept the responsibility of implementing the policies, laws and interventions they deem appropriate to counter the phenomenon, and to respect the obligations they hold as signatories to the international drug control conventions.

All this means that it is difficult to consider the convergence of national policies as a direct consequence of the EU's involvement and action. In this respect, it is not easy for us to support the hypothesis of a strict Europeanization of national drug policies as has been the case in other policy fields where, for instance, the EU has clear competencies and the power to enforce binding instruments and implement policies. But this conclusion is not in conflict with a more general observation that the EU may have nevertheless contributed more indirectly to this convergence through what political scientists call 'soft instruments' such as action plans, strategies, recommendations or Council resolutions. For instance, we could identify in this regard EU strategies and action plans on drugs that foresee specific objectives and targets and that, while fully respecting the subsidiarity principle, encourage member states to implement interventions that tackle the drug phenomenon. Even though they are not binding, these instruments attempt to provide a guide to all actors in the EU when setting priorities in the drugs area.

The successive EU strategies and action plans on drugs that have existed for 15 years are an effort towards more coordination between the member states and the EU institutions. And as we noted earlier, the founding of the EMCDDA has contributed to the harmonization of the way the phenomenon has been monitored and reported. In itself, this has influenced the selection of the issues and policy priorities to be tackled. Overall, the existence of these structures and the opportunities for the sharing of perspectives and experiences has supported policy transfers from one member state to another.

Conclusion

If we have seen a drift towards a more common approach to what has become a more common problem, the question that remains to be answered is whether this process will continue further. Here it is difficult to speculate, since cooperation on supply reduction measures and border control has become a more complex and important debate because of the overlap with money-laundering and heightened concerns about security and terrorism. With respect to discussions on drug demand, historically the health agenda and issues concerning HIV tended to be central. Increasingly, however, concerns over relationship of drug use to criminality and public security and safety are becoming important topics and a focus for drug policy debate. Emergence of the public nuisance issue is one example of this, drugs and driving and drug testing are others.

The integration of ten new member states has also altered the picture somewhat. The growth in problem heroin use and HIV infection remain important issues in the new member states. And some of these new European countries are now threatened by the most rapidly developing HIV epidemic in the world. Drug problems tend to coalesce with other social ills and can disproportionately affect societies going through social and economic change. Moreover, Europe's borders now directly embrace the Russian

Federation and some of the former soviet republics. These are areas of the world where both injecting drug use and HIV infection are causing considerable concern and where new trafficking routes have developed, or have the potential to develop. The new member states have been quick to embrace some aspects of the European drug policy perspective as part of the accession process. For example, HIV rates remain low in most countries and HIV prevention measures are now given a relatively high priority in some. In Estonia and Latvia there has been a dramatically increased investment in prevention measures that is now possibly contributing to the fall in newly-diagnosed HIV infections. However, in many countries compared with Europe as a whole, services for drug users remain underdeveloped and the political debate on drug issues is more volatile.

As well as differences between countries it is also possible to identify groups of countries who appear to differ from the rest on aspects of drug policy. For example, the Nordic countries, the Mediterranean countries, the Baltic countries and the new member states. All could at some level be described as having a distinctive perspective. Nonetheless, despite this heterogeneity it is also now possible to find support for the hypothesis that there exists a common set of policy principles that are shared by most, if not all, EU countries and a common implementation of interventions and practices throughout Europe. There is considerable variation with respect to balance of elements within individual countries' strategies and how they are implemented. When European member states meet to specifically discuss drug issues they may have points of controversy and disagreement – heroin distribution and supervised consumption rooms being two current examples. However, for the most part, these controversies are more about detail than fundamentals. In short, countries are still different but not as much as they were before and, while policies differ, they do so within a common if somewhat broad overall perspective that some commentators have referred to as the 'European model for drug policy'.

References

Bergeron, H. (2005a) Europeanisation of drug policies: from common principles to mutual agreement, *in* M. Steffen and J. Lehto (eds) *Europeanisation of Health Policies: Issues, Challenges, Innovations*. London: Routledge.

Bergeron, H. (2005b) Les politiques publiques en Europe: de l'ordre à la santé publique, *in* P. Reynaud (ed.) *Médecines et Addictions*. Paris: Edition Masson.

Bergeron, H. (2005c) Drogues, risques et société, *in* M. Steffen (ed.) *Risques et Société*. Paris: L'Harmattan.

Berridge, V. and Stanton, J. (1999) Science and policy: historical insights, *Social Science and Medicine*, special issue, Science Speaks to Policy, 49: 1113–38.

Bless, R. (2003) Experiences of the multi-city network of the Pompidou Group, 1983–2002, *Bulletin of Narcotics*, 1 & 2: 31–40.

EMCDDA (2005a) *Annual report 2004: The State of the Drugs Problem in the European Union and Norway.* Lisbon: EMCDDA.

EMCDDA (2005b) *Illicit Drug Use in the EU: Legislative Approaches.* Lisbon: thematic paper, EMCDDA.

European Commission (1999) *Communication from the Commission to the Council and European Parliament on a European Union Action Plan to Combat Drugs (2000–2004).* Brussels: European Commission.

Hartnoll, R. (2003) Drug epidemiology in the European institutions: historical background and key indicators, *Bulletin of Narcotics*, 1 & 2: 31–40.

Musto, D. and Sloboda, Z. (2003) The influence of epidemiology on drug control policy, *Bulletin of Narcotics*, 1 & 2: 9–22.

Zobel, F., Ramstein, T. and Arnaud, S. (2004) *Les interventions publiques nationales en matière d'abus de substances et de dépendances : une revue internationale.* Lausanne: Institut Universitaire de Médecine Sociale et Préventive.

Further reading

Albrecht, H-J. and van Kalmthout, A. (eds) (1989) *Drug Policies in Western Europe. Criminological Research.*

Berridge, V. (1996) European Drug Policy: The Need for Historical Perspectives. *European Addiction Research*, 2: 219–25.

Boekout, Van Solinge T. (2005) *Dealing with Drugs in Europe.* The Hague: BJU Legal Publishers.

Cattacin, S. and Lucas, B. (1999) Autorégulation, intervention étatique, mise en réseau. Les transformations de l'Etat social en Europe. Les cas du VIH/SIDA, de l'abus d'alcool et des drogues illégales, *Revue Française de Sciences Politiques*, 49: 379–98.

Eisner, M. (1997) Determinant of Swiss drug policy: the case of the heroin prescription program, *Deviance and Society*, 23: 189–204.

Tham, H. (1995) Drug control as a national project: the case of Sweden, *Journal of Drug Issues*, 25: 113–28.

chapter

nine

Contemporary Social Theory in the Drugs Field

Paul Higate

Introduction

It has been argued that contemporary social theory represents an under-utilized resource in drugs policy and social policy (Carter *et al.* 1998; Coffey 2004; Duff 2004: 386). On the occasions when social theory has been used in drug research, however, it has 'tended to focus on method rather than theory' (Moore and Rhodes 2004: 324). There are other reasons for the relative neglect of theory in the drugs field, including those relating to the demands of the policy process. For example, researchers are frequently under pressure to produce 'policy friendly' quantitative data,[1] although qualitative data has increasingly come to be seen as a useful resource for policy-makers (Measham *et al.* 1998).

Discussion in this chapter is informed by a recent special issue of the *International Journal of Drugs Policy* (*IJDP*) (2004) in which contributions illustrate the utility of contemporary social theory to the field of drugs policy and research. Theory discussed in the *IJDP* has focused on: social capital, governmentality, poststructuralism, embodiment, consumption, spatiality, cultural geography, discourse analysis, risk and structure, and agency (Moore and Rhodes 2004: 323). The co-editors of the *IJDP* argue that it is important to disseminate new theory (Moore and Rhodes 2004: 323), not least because the rapidly evolving social context of the policy arena demands fresh perspectives with which to throw light on the complex interactions of human agency and the shifting cultures of drug use (Shiner and Newburn 1999; Bunton 2001). A number of the concepts used in the *IJDP* are elaborated and discussed below.

---

1 The government's key performance indicators (such as those based on drug testing) rely on quantitative units of assessment.

This chapter is organized in the following way. In terms of social context, postmodernity is considered with a focus on interpretations that have highlighted consumer capitalism, lifestyle, identity and drugs. Drawing on commentators who have discussed risk in the drugs field and more widely, it is argued that policy-makers frame drug users as essentially rational. Here, drug users' (apparent) aversion to risk is seen as lying dormant, to be awakened through exposure to the appropriate information concerning the risks of substance use. Prior to a brief overview of research in the drugs field that has taken space and place as its point of departure, I signal the importance of embodying drug use. The chapter concludes with a brief summary, together with reflection on the importance of analysing the social-structural context of drug use. The focus on the context of drug use is intended to complement and develop skewed approaches that have tended to concentrate on the individualized pathologies of drug users on the one hand, or the pharmacological effects of the substances they use on the other.

The social context

Postmodernity and consumer capitalism

One of the most controversial concepts to emerge within the social sciences over the last two decades is that of postmodernity. This over-used concept has arisen in discussions concerning drugs in relation to consumer culture. In our contemporary form of consumer capitalism, lifestyle and identity have come to be grounded in the cultures of everyday life with, as a growing number of commentators have suggested, the pursuit of pleasure at its nexus (Ruggerio 1999; Shiner and Newburn 1999; South 1999). The concept of postmodernity and its equivalents, 'late modernity', 'high modernity' (Giddens 1991) and 'liquid modernity' (Bauman 2000) could be seen as sensitizing concepts, or shorthand for the rapidly transforming social context of drug use, particularly in respect of consumerism. From film, through media to books, literature and art, consciousness-altering substances have long been co-opted into the constantly innovating techniques and limitless products of the dynamic free market, pervading the most unlikely of spheres. This saturation of lifestyle culture with drugs appears to have intensified in recent years, provoking one commentator to suggest that the 'rave new world' has arrived (Blackman 2004).

Set within this cultural context, the relative failure of policy to curb the volume of drugs ingested by (particularly) younger members of the population (Shiner and Newburn 1999) may not come as news to many. After all, it is counter-intuitive to imagine that pleasure substances would be shunned in a culture where there is a celebrated congruence between what we consume and how we are perceived by self and others. 'Drugs', as van Ree has stated are ' "luxury" *pur sang*,[2] the ideal typical product of the consumer society' (2002: 351). And as Hart and Carter (2000: 236) suggest in relation to the symbolic resonance of drug use:

> Consumption . . . is not simply concerned with the purchase of material commodities but refers also to broader 'lifestyle' choices and practices including ideas, beliefs, attitudes and desires . . . the social meanings which become attached to commodities are seen as important to shaping individuals' identities.

For many, consumer culture trumps the message of prevention and the mechanisms of punishment. As Blackman suggests (2004: 52): 'Government, as one branch of the state, gives out a singular message of drug prohibition, but in free market capitalism we find a range of drug representations employed by entrepreneurs to capture a market'. Commentators have also turned their attention to the so-called risk society (Beck 1992), arguing that our 'precarious freedoms' in contemporary times signal an important transformation, not so much in terms of postmodernity but rather 'a second modernity' (Beck 1992; Hart and Carter 2000: 241).

Risk society

In our contemporary 'knowledge society', it is argued that 'Risk is no longer about private fears of the random unknown. It now involves public perception of universal dangerousness and threat' (Culpitt 1999: 4). Discourses of risk circulate in different spheres from routine conversation through to political discourse. One important subtext of the risk discourse is that individuals – conceived of in neo-liberal or free market terms – are understood to be naturally risk-averse and rational in the face of potential harm to their well-being. By making the right 'choice', and by assimilating and acting on appropriate information, negotiating risk, it is suggested, becomes a process of calculation embedded into reflexive social practice (Giddens 1991; Beck 1992). As Jones suggests: 'much social policy interprets risk as the matter of responsibility, prudent choice and the individual calculus of advantage' (2004: 369).

The term 'risk society' has had a significant impact across the social sciences, and for some years has been incorporated into theoretical and empirical work within the drugs field (MacGregor 1999; O'Malley 1999; Ruggerio 1999; Bunton 2001; Peretti-Watel 2003; Jones 2004). Analysis has included a focus on the political context of risk discourse in respect of government informed drug policies in many countries including the UK (Jones 2004) and Australia (O'Malley 1999; Duff 2003). For example,

---

2 The literal translation from French is 'thoroughbred'.

Jones (2004: 368) has highlighted the saturation of policy statements in the UK with the language of risk.

Duff (2003) has been critical of Australian drug policy under the Howard government because of the shift from policies of harm minimization to zero tolerance. Here, drugs have been framed as the source of harm, rather than the ways in which they are used. As Duff states (2003: 287): 'With the locus of risk found in the pharmacology of the substance . . . it is argued that the principal aim of any risk management strategy becomes the minimisation of the consumption of these substances'.

Policies supporting harm minimization approaches in Australia and in other countries originate from expert discourses. It is here that risk policy relies almost solely on risk or prevention 'science'. Duff (2003) details the extent to which risk management discourses generated at the governmental-policy level may fail to resonate with drug users or, in Beck's (Beck and Beck-Gernsheim 1996) parlance, the 'lay actors' themselves. Thus, the risks articulated at the level of policy discourse associated with cannabis use in the Australian context are drawn from studies detailing heavy and protracted use. The spurious presentation of these consumption patterns as the norm neglects the diversity of ways, and different contexts in which, cannabis is consumed over time and between cultures. This leads Duff (2003: 289) to suggest that 'the science of risk . . . ignores the array of social norms, rituals and customs' associated with the use of this and other substances. Drug users' experience can tend to be treated as a kind of untested knowledge, and consequently accorded little credibility by drug policy-makers. In these terms, drug users may be conceived of as irrational, though likely to act rationally or appropriately when equipped with the appropriate knowledge or guidance.[3]

In the UK, attempts have been made to develop social relationships between younger potential users together with a focus on building assertive-ness, self-esteem and resistance to advertising and peer pressure (Jones 2004). Perhaps more encouragingly, there is growing recognition that the starting point for effective policy is to understand better the 'existing knowledge, experience and perceptions of drug issues' from young people themselves (Jones 2004: 370). However, educational programmes continue to focus on behaviour modification and risk management and in so doing frame drug users as rationally calculating beings within the context of risk as 'negative'. Yet, there is much to be learned from research in the drugs field that takes 'risk-as-positive' as its prime point of departure – for example, within the context of drug-taking in the rave scene (Hutton 2004); here, and in other contexts, risk may act as a catalyst to use (Collison 1996).

---

3 See Rhodes (1995) for an interesting discussion of the role of social theory in respect of the 'conscious and calculated' versus 'ritualised and habituated' practices of needle-sharing drug users.

An important critique of drug policy that focuses on risk and its corollary, the rational drug user, is that it can often fail to locate individuals in their social or cultural contexts. As Hart and Carter (2000: 242) argue in relation to HIV/AIDS and risk behaviour: 'The process of reflexive modernisation . . . may only be found in limited cultural contexts [and for some drug users] the scope for therapeutic "choice", "empowerment" or "reflexivity"[4] is severely limited'. Drug users, particularly those experiencing social exclusion, are likely to be ill equipped to negotiate the daily challenges that shape, and are shaped by, problem drug use. These individuals may be imbued by policy-makers with a wholly unrealistic capacity for transformative social practice that may call on them (for example), to develop a non-drug using social network. This profound shift in social networks is unlikely to be achieved in the absence of considerable levels of sustained support that are currently lacking, as Joanne Neale argues in Chapter 1.

Drug users as embodied

As we have seen, lay actors considered as rational in negotiating the harms associated with drug use continue to be important to the ideological underpinning of recent and current drug policy (Newcombe and Parry 1989; Stimson and Lart 1991). In foregrounding the role of rationality in drug use, harm minimization policies appeal to the reasonable thinking of drug users. Here, policy implicitly conceives of the actions of drug users as located in mind and cognition, and in so doing ignores the role of embodiment in these activities.[5] However, over the last decade, sociologists have begun to consider the role of the physical body or the corporeal self in shaping social practice. Their argument is that physical bodies are sentient[6] and should not be ignored when attempting to explain many aspects of everyday life. Approaches that consider the body analytically develop one aspect of contemporary social theory that aims to move beyond the simplistic rational actor or Cartesian models of human agency. As the sociologist Shilling (1997: 745) argues: 'Socialization needs analysing in terms of the partial social shaping of embodied dispositions as well as in terms of the partial internalization of mental views and attitudes' (1997: 45).

4 In simple terms, reflexivity refers to the ways in which individuals are required to come to terms with the fast-moving, information-rich environment of the modern world. Failure to 'keep up' with the rapid pace of change set against the retrenchment of welfare, fuels an increasingly sharp polarization between reflexivity 'winners' and reflexivity 'losers'.

5 If we consider that bodies are in part cultural artefacts, then it is important to acknowledge related ways of thinking about the drug-culture-body link. In the following quote concerning HIV/AIDS, 'culture' can be seen as interchangeable with 'bodies': 'If future research is to maintain a practical contribution to the design and implementation of harm reduction intervention, then a primary focus of such research has to be the interaction between cognition and *culture*' (Rhodes and Stimson 1994: 220).

6 Thinking about the body as sentient requires an imaginative leap such that we come to understand bodies as having lives of their own *outside* rational or willed action.

It is then, within a post-Cartesian nexus linking the body, society and the mind that useful insights might be generated regarding drug use as an exemplary *embodied* social practice (Ettorre 2004: 30).[7] Within the context of drug addiction, for example, it is suggested that: 'While the ostensible *symptoms* of addiction overwhelmingly consist in social or cultural transgression, its underlying *nature* is generally located in one or another sort of bodily pathology, deficit or vulnerability' (Weinberg 2002: 1). Weinberg critiques a number of theories currently used to explain addiction,[8] in order to provide conceptual space for the embodied dimensions of problem drug use. In attempting to explain what some might see as a kind of irrationality signalled through craving, he poses the following question: 'What is it about some people's drug experiences that fosters powerful visceral cravings even after repeated associating of drug use with negative experiences?' (2002: 11). Thus, rather than understanding addiction as rooted solely in the mind and cognition, Weinberg (2002: 14) argues for a consideration of the 'prereflective, non symbolic and embodied' components of human agency. He says: 'By learning through practice to participate in social activities, people come to personally embody culturally transmitted meanings at a *pre-reflective*, or habitual, level of being' (*emphasis added*).

People act in ways, and in relation to objects, that *precede* meaning, or processes of rational decision-making. In attempting to make sense of what appears to be 'uncalculated and involuntary' action, it is helpful to consider the embodiment of human agency (Weinberg 2002: 15). In this way, an important (and elusive) component of addiction may be understood as embodied, 'beyond the self' and unrelated to the exercise of 'free will'. By 'bringing in the body', we are able to contribute towards a greater understanding of the sophistication of human agency, including a recognition that individuals' social practices unfold in ways that appear to be unrelated to their exercise of free will. Bodies are malleable and change through time. They are shaped by ritual and, within the context of addiction, may provide clues to a particular activity that has become habitualized and sedimented into the embodied dimensions of social practice.

The role of space and place

The terms 'space' and 'place' have formed the intellectual building blocks for a disciplinary enterprise that has resonated across the social sciences in human geography, cultural studies and sociology (Hubbard *et al.* 2004: 1–15). Empirical and theoretical work has explored how space, place and

---

7   An alternative focus on the body in the drugs literature concerns the ways in which drug-using bodies might be controlled or examined.

8   Weinberg analyses three theories of addiction. He considers neurological explanations, social learning theories and finally, symbolic interactionist theories. The limitations of each theory are considered within the context of their over-reliance on the mind and cognition.

social relations interact with one another, helping to influence particular cultural practices. Space is usually understood as the arena 'in which social relations and identity are constituted' whereas place has tended to be conceptualized as the 'individual's attachments to particular [places] . . . which link events . . . and attitudes to create a fused whole' (Duncan 2000: 582–4). In the drugs field, the concepts of space and place have been used innovatively to explore pleasure, surveillance and cultures of drug use.[9] Theorizing informed by the spatial perspective might be relevant to understanding the deeply embodied experiential and pre-verbal aspects of recreational drug use, including those developing through dance in the club scene:

> Drug spaces are smooth, full of intensities ebbing and flowing; of the forces of music, sex, touch and sensuality moving through the body; of nothing located; of nothing specific. Rather, a general series of waves that move off along planes into new spaces. The body, not being a destination or an origin, is simply another becoming possibility in a manifold space.
> (Slavin 2004: 289)

The phrase 'head space' has been used to signal drug users' desire to achieve 'a controlled loss of control' in an increasingly stressful world. Here, it is argued that drugs can facilitate 'time out' in bounded (regulated and unregulated) locations (Measham 2004: 343–4; see also MacAndrew and Edgerton 1969). In doing so, drugs can provide a brief reprieve or escape from the mundanity of paramount reality,[10] the ritualized experiences of which may come to be linked with particular spaces and places. Most of the recent literature in the drugs field using space as its point of departure has focused on the unique environment of the club and sexual identity.

Club spaces

The idea of 'tribal space' has been used to develop illustrative insights into drug use in a gay club in the Australian city of Sydney. In this ethnographic account of a night in the club, there is an attempt to 'explore the social possibilities of drug use within particular spatial circumstances' by describing

---

9 The terms 'set' (referring to the personality of the drug user) and 'setting' (the social context of drug use) have been widely used within the drugs literature to make sense of the drug experience (see Zinberg 1974 for a classic rendition). There is a sense in which the *social setting* of drug use resonates with a more developed discourse in terms of the links between *space* and drug use, sketched briefly in the current chapter. Importantly, the terms social setting and space/place are both considered in terms of their productive force in shaping the nature of the drug experience.

10 According to Cohen and Taylor (1992), as members of modern societies we are confronted by a 'life plan' that is defined and maintained by bureaucratic agencies. This is our dominant or 'paramount reality', an ever-present challenge to our sense of self-determination and individuality. Escape attempts (e.g. the use of drugs) are strategies to evade the routines of a predictable life plan.

'the ways that space and sociality interact, dynamically performing and producing each other' (Slavin 2004: 268). This contribution recognizes that spatiality is central to illicit drug use and could be included in policy thinking, particularly harm reduction strategies. Slavin suggests that while drug use may be common among gay men in Sydney, nevertheless it tends to occur in spaces where the management of its meanings can be ritualistically handled (2004: 275). In this way, drugs are argued to be problematic only 'when used in spaces that lack structuring elements or when a culture of use has not sufficiently developed' (2004: 288). Use of drugs in this particular club in Sydney is understood in these terms as normalized and governed by informal rules. Here, the risks from drugs are countered through codes of acceptable versus excessive use within the context of a shared sociality in the club space (Shiner and Newburn 1999).

Drug spaces: inside and outside

The spaces of both the club and the city have been used to consider the changing nature of leisure sites in regard to the use of legal and illicit drug use. For example, the emergence of the commercial 'super-club' in the UK represents a recent development set against the: '[O]utdoor (licensed and unlicensed) "alternative" music festivals and raves . . . which reflected the dual fortunes of the mainstream and the underground in popular culture' (Measham 2004: 338). The split between indoors and outdoors, it has been suggested, reflected a commercially sanctioned space in the former, with outdoors understood as providing the 'pursuit of forbidden and unpredictable sense of place' in the latter (cited in Measham 2004: 339). Now that super-clubs are in decline, the search has reverted to more intimate, less impersonal surroundings. However, from the mid-1990s, it has been suggested that two strands of dance space had developed – commercialization and criminalization. Unlicensed raves were subject to increasing legislation and considered as risky spaces, framed through health and safety discourse, when contrasted with the increasingly regulated and licensed clubs located in urban centres (Measham 2004). Yet, somewhat ironically, the move from unregulated (outdoor) to regulated (indoor) spaces may have *exacerbated* the harms associated with the use of dance drugs:

> The addition of a roof and four walls had alarming consequences. Overheating had rarely been a significant risk in the fields, caves, beaches and disused warehouses of the early acid house era, but the move to indoor, commercial club space changed the drug setting . . . medical studies suggested that the casualties of the rave scene appeared to be related to dance drug-related pharmacological and environmental complications such as heat-stroke, dehydration and hyponatraemia.
>
> (Measham 2004: 341)

Since the late 1990s, policies have been developed to manage the risks associated with indoor dance venues that have worked with the grain of particular drug cultures, while over the same period, patterns of drug use and type of substance used have evolved with alcohol moving back into favour. The city as the prime space for consumption, and alcohol as a widely and creatively promoted intoxicator now coexist in ways that have further supplanted the unlicensed outdoor 'play space' of the 1990s.

Spaces of governance

A further contribution that draws on the concept of space within the context of the risks associated with drug use concerns the use of 'supervised injecting sites' (SIS) for intravenous drug use (IDU) (Fischer *et al.* 2004: 357). While these sites represent formalized spaces linked to policies of harm reduction, they also stand for spaces in which the socially excluded individual (in this case the user of opiates) can be separated from other (non-deviant) members in the urban setting. Individuals using these sites can therefore be carefully disciplined and placed under surveillance. These disciplining technologies couch the user as 'an agent of risk related to health' (Fischer *et al.* 2004: 358), and represent a further example of the governance of drug users in contemporary society. Drug-related activities in the club space (as I argue above) are shaped by self-governing social practice, whereas similar activities in the space of the SIS are normatively influenced by external factors aimed at encouraging safe injecting practices. The establishment of SIS represents a good example of the so-called 'dual city', the spaces of which are configured through the inclusion or exclusion of certain groups designated as deviant or otherwise. Importantly in terms of policy, drug users may be reluctant to use the space of the SIS as, echoing discussions above in regard to lay perceptions of risk, they may not feel safe and comfortable in rule-bound sites controlled by 'professionals': '[I]t appears that many IDU decline the offer to [use] SIS, since their design and rules may express mainly others' concepts of "safety" and comfort and not their own, and deny them practices to remedy these shortcomings' (Fischer *et al.*, 2004: 360). Here, drug users are noted to resist practices (determined by powerful others) monitoring the SIS. Resistance may be linked to these individuals' sense of having little or no input into the architectural design and operation of particular spaces in which they are transformed from volitional into 'docile bodies'.[11]

11 The term 'docile bodies' was coined by the French theorist Michel Foucault (1977) as a way to show how surveillance and power combine to create passivity.

Degraded spaces: 'out there'

In attempting to reconcile the tensions between addiction 'as a disease' whereby users are 'chronically enslaved' by forces beyond themselves, and the demands that they *control* their use while in therapy programmes, Weinberg (2000) has drawn on space as a symbolic point of departure. Here, the phrase 'out there' is used by addicts who frame 'the streets' as the backdrop to the degraded culture with which they have become associated through their drug use. This savage environment has been described as a place of temptation, fuelling problem drug users' slide into addiction. As Weinberg suggests (2000: 611): 'the self destructive behavior of active addicts was held to be caused not only by an intra-personal "disease", but also by the decidedly despised ecological space that was held to sustain and exacerbate that disease'. Here, spatial discourses invoking drug culture rely on binary thinking; drug-using spaces are consistently bracketed out of 'normal society'; they are out there, dirty, risky or hedonistic. By implication, these spaces of transgression are accorded powers sufficient to shape human agency. They are spaces of production, held to exert a powerful influence over the courses of action and possibilities open to those described as, and self-identifying as, addicts.

Gendered space

In this final section, qualitative research exploring constructions of femininity and risk in club spaces of late 1990s northern England is discussed[12] (Hutton 2004). It has already been pointed out that club spaces are culturally diverse in terms of sexuality and drug norms together with the extent to which they might be described as mainstream or underground. Drawing attention to the informal rules that shape, and are shaped by, club goers, one participant in Hutton's study suggested: 'If I were to drop into (names club) I would stick out like a sore thumb, not being fifteen, six stone and going out in my underwear! Different types of clubs and different types of music, it tends to split off into loads of different crowds and people can easily identify who their pack members are' ('Cynthia' cited in Hutton 2004: 226).

One of a number of social practices shaped by club spaces is that constituting gendered relations. Here, mainstream clubs can be perceived as 'meat markets', or as spaces in which women endure sexist approaches from drunken males described as 'sexually threatening' (Hutton 2004: 227). In these mainstream clubs, hetero-normative cultures predominate, shaping acceptable sexualities (heterosexual), and those deemed deviant (homosexual). However, in terms of risk, many of the female participants in the

---

12 Hutton's (2004) study included interviews with 26 women between the ages of 21 and 39, many of whom had been involved in clubbing between the late 1980s and early 1990s. She also used ethnographic methods in clubs in Manchester, Sheffield and Leeds.

study argued that because they had used ecstasy (and perhaps other drugs), a number of men perceived them as 'up for it sexually' (Hutton 2004: 228). In addition, the drugs of choice in these spaces (alcohol/mainstream and ecstasy/underground) also played a role in shaping how participants were able to negotiate safe sex. Discussing the participants in the study, Hutton (p. 230) states: 'There was . . . a shared view that alcohol far more than drugs made women take risks . . . taking E made them retain more control and be more assertive about sex and condom use'.

In relation to gendered relations and sexuality it was suggested that:

> Club spaces may allow for more equality between the sexes, but difference is still apparent. This difference changes, and can become more or less, according to what kind of club space women are negotiating their sexualities in. Some types of clubbing events are seen as safer than others, so sexualities can be negotiated within wider parameters. Male attitudes within differing spaces are an important factor in how 'free' women attending feel.
>
> (Hutton 2004: 234)

In sum, Hutton's study elaborates risk within the context of sexuality and sexual practice, conceived of through the lens of space and place. Given that common sense explanations continue to focus on the individual pathologies of drug users, or alternatively, the pharmacological properties of substances (or a mixture of both), it is useful to broaden analysis to consider the productive role of space and place in the social relations of problem and recreational drug use.

Concluding comments

In this chapter, I have introduced readers to a range of concepts that have begun to exert an influence on theorizing in the drugs field. The intention has been to highlight the topicality of particular concepts rather than to argue for their distinct novelty, though some theoretical innovation is apparent particularly regarding the embodiment of drug use, for example.

First, the concept of postmodernity was considered with regard to the ways in which it might sensitize us to our current stage of consumer capitalism, turning on the importance of lifestyle and identity. Second, the theme of risk was discussed within the context of risk society, and the ways in which drug policy might frame drug users as rationally calculating in their negotiation of harms. Third, arguments were presented in which the embodiment of human agency was considered as a contribution to the explanations of the apparent 'irrationality' of drug use. The sentience of the body, it was suggested, should not be disregarded when considering the complex nature of 'flesh and tissue' social practice. Finally, the concepts of space and place were considered as a way to signal the productive power of particular settings. The language of space and place can be used to complement earlier work focusing on the 'drug setting', an important factor in drug users' risk behaviour, and other practices linked to substance use.

It is hoped that the attempts in this chapter to synthesize aspects of an emerging literature dealing with social theory in the drugs field may motivate interested readers to make use of theoretically innovative ideas in their own work. In starting from an understanding that individuals – be they drug users or otherwise – might appear to act in contradictory or irrational ways, we might usefully consider their embodied and spatialized social practices. These ways of conceptualizing drug users and drug use, while not immediately reconcilable with the policy interface, nevertheless are vital if we are to move towards understanding the complexities of both problem and recreational drug use in contemporary society.

References

Bauman, Z. (2000) *Liquid Modernity*. Cambridge: Polity Press.

Beck, U. (1992) *Risk Society: Towards a New Modernity*. London: Sage.

Beck, U. and Beck-Gernsheim, E. (1996) Individualization and 'precarious freedoms': perspectives and controversies of a subject-oriented sociology, in P. Heelas, S. Lash and P. Morris (eds) *Detraditionalization*. London: Blackwell.

Blackman, S. (2004) *Chilling Out: The Cultural Politics of Substance Consumption, Youth and Drug Policy*. Maidenhead: Open University Press.

Bunton, R. (2001) Knowledge, embodiment and neo-liberal drug policy, *Contemporary Drug Problems*, 28: 221–43.

Carter, J. (ed.) (1998) *Postmodernity and the Fragmentation of Welfare*. London: Routledge.

Coffey, A. (2004) *Reconceptualizing Social Policy*. Maidenhead: Open University Press.

Cohen, S. and Taylor, L. (1992) *Escape Attempts*. London: Routledge.

Collison, M. (1996) In search of the high life: drugs, crime, masculinities and consumption, *British Journal of Criminology*, 36(3): 428–44.

Culpitt, I. (1999) *Social Policy and Risk*. London: Sage.

Duff, C. (2003) The importance of culture and context: rethinking risk and risk management in young drug using populations, *Health, Risk & Society*, 5: 285–99.

Duff, C. (2004) Drug use as a 'practice of the self': is there any place for an 'ethics of moderation' in contemporary drug policy? *International Journal of Drug Policy*, 15: 385–93.

Duncan, J. (2000) 'Place', in R. J. Johnston, D. Gregory, G. Pratt and M. Watts (eds) *The Dictionary of Human Geography*. London: Blackwell.

Ettorre, E. (2004) Revisioning women and drug use: gender sensitivity, embodiment and reducing harm, *International Journal of Drug Policy*, 15: 327–55.

Fischer, B., Turnbull, S.D., Poland, B. and Haydon, E. (2004) Drug use, risk and urban order: examining supervised injection sites (SISs) as governmentality, *International Journal of Drug Policy*, 15: 357–65.

Foucault, M. (1977) *Discipline and Punish*. London: Penguin.

Giddens, A. (1991) *Modernity and Self Identity*. Cambridge: Polity Press.

Hart, G. and Carter, S. (2000) Drugs and risk: developing a sociology of HIV risk behaviour, in S. Williams, J. Gabe and M. Calnan (eds) *Health, Medicine and Society: Key Theories, Future Agendas*. London: Routledge.

Hubbard, P., Kitchin, R. and Valentine, G. (2004) Editor's introduction: key thinkers on space and place, in P. Hubbard, R. Kitchin and G. Valentine (eds) *Key Thinkers on Space and Place*. London: Sage.

Hutton, F. (2004) Up for it, mad for it? Women, drug use and participation in club scenes, *Health, Risk and Society*, 6: 223–7.

Jones, M. (2004) Anxiety and containment in the risk society: theorising young people and drug prevention policy, *International Journal of Drug Policy*, 15: 367–76.

MacAndrew, C. and Edgerton, R.B. (1969) *Drunken Comportment: A Social Explanation*. Chicago: Aldine.

MacGregor, S. (1999) Medicine, custom or moral fibre: policy responses to drug misuse, in N. South (ed.) *Drugs: Cultures, Controls & Everyday Life*. London: Sage.

Measham, F. (2004) Play space: historical and socio-cultural reflections on drugs, licensed leisure locations, commercialisation and control, *International Journal of Drugs Policy*, 15: 337–45.

Measham, F., Parker, H. and Aldridge, J. (1998) *Starting, Switching, Slowing and Stopping*. London: Home Office.

Moore, D. and Rhodes, T. (2004) Editorial: social theory in drug research, drug policy and harm reduction, *International Journal of Drug Policy*, 15: 323–5.

Newcombe, R. and Parry, A. (1989) *Preventing the Spread of HIV Infection Among and from Injecting Drug Users in the UK: An Overview with Specific Reference to the Mersey Regional Strategy* (mimeo). Liverpool: Mersey Regional Health Authority.

O'Malley, P. (1999) Consuming risks: harm minimization and the government of 'drug-users', in R. Smandych (ed.) *Governable Places*. Aldershot: Ashgate.

Peretti-Watel, P. (2003) Neutralization theory and the denial of risk: some evidence from cannabis use among French adolescents, *British Journal of Sociology*, 1: 21–42.

Rhodes, D. and Stimson, G. (1994) What is the relationship between drug taking and sexual risk? *Sociology of Health and Illness*, 16: 209–29.

Rhodes, T. (1995) Theorising and researching 'risk': notes on the social relations of risk in heroin users' lifestyles, in P. Aggleton, P. Davies and G. Hart (eds) *AIDS: Safety, Sexuality and Risk*. London: Taylor & Francis.

Ruggerio, V. (1999) Drugs as a password and the law as a drug: discussing the legalisation of illicit substances, in N. South (ed.) *Drugs: Cultures, Controls & Everyday Life*. London: Sage.

Shilling, C. (1997) The undersocialized conception of the embodied agent in modern sociology, *Sociology*, 31: 737–54.

Shiner, M. and Newburn, T. (1999) Taking tea with Noel: the place and meaning of drug use in everyday life, in N. South (ed.) *Drugs: Cultures, Controls & Everyday Life*. London: Sage.

Slavin, S. (2004) Drugs, space, and sociality in a gay nightclub in Sydney, *Journal of Contemporary Ethnography*, 33: 265–95.

South, N. (1999) Debating drugs and everyday life: normalisation, prohibition and 'otherness', in N. South (ed.) *Drugs: Cultures, Controls & Everyday Life*. London: Sage.

Stimson, G. and Lart, R. (1991) HIV, drugs and public health in England: new words, old tunes, *The International Journal of the Addictions*, 26: 1263–77.

van Ree, E. (2002) Drugs, the democratic civilising process and the consumer society, *International Journal of Drug Policy*, 13: 349–53.

Weinberg, D. (2000) Out there: the ecology of addiction in drug abuse treatment discourse, *Social Problems*, 47: 606–21.

Weinberg, D. (2002) On the embodiment of addiction, *Body & Society*, 8: 1–19.

Zinberg, N.E. (1974) *Drug, Set and Setting*. Newhaven, CT: Yale University Press.

Further reading

Burkitt, I. (1999) *Bodies of Thought: Social Relations, Activity and Embodiment*. London: Sage.

Low, S.M. and Lawrence-Zeniga, D. (2003) *The Anthropology of Space and Place: Locating Culture*. London: Blackwell.

Woods, T. (1999) *Beginning Postmodernism*. Manchester: Manchester University Press.

Young, J. (1971) *The Drugtakers*. London: Paladin.

Index